CW00693240

HARDPRESS.NET
HOME OF HARD-TO-FIND BOOKS

A Statement of the Trinitarian Principle, or Law of Tri-Personality
by Unknown

Address:
HardPress
8345 NW 66TH ST #2561
MIAMI FL 33166-2626
USA
Email: info@hardpress.net

ZFGC
ANNEX

A

STATEMENT

OF THE

TRINITARIAN PRINCIPLE,

OR

LAW OF TRI-PERSONALITY.

Ephraim Langdon

"For there are three that bear record in heaven, the Father, the Word,
and the Holy Ghost: and these three are One.

And there are three that bear witness in earth, the Spirit, the Water,
and the Blood: and these three agree in One."

1 JOHN, 5: 7, 8.

BOSTON:

JOHN P. JEWETT AND COMPANY,

17 and 19 Cornhill.

1853.

PRINTED BY PRENTISS AND SAWYER,
No. 11 Devonshire Street.

INTRODUCTION.

THE following statement of the Trinitarian Principle, or Law of Tri-Personality, was made by the writer many years since as the foundation of a Universal Science, or form of Universal Philosophy; a work that has since then occupied a portion of his time, and which he is now preparing for publication, as " *The Marriage of Philosophy and Faith.*"

The statement here made is a logical argument based upon *self-evident truths* demonstrating that fact of Tri-Personality in God which has always been assumed dogmatically by the Church as the foundation of its theology; but which being, as there stated, poetical, and not rational, could not serve as a foundation for Philosophy, or even as a *permanent* basis for Theology. Although the foundation upon which this statement of Tri-Personality rests is partly hypothetical, as it is also *self-evident*, this logical demonstration ought to be regarded as sufficient, and the Law of Tri-Personality thus established be received without question as the only true ground of Philosophy, and the only rational foundation for Christian Theology. It is not, however,

upon this internal evidence alone that we intend to rest
our statement. Being founded in Universal Laws of
Being, which can be illustrated by all the phenomena
of natural existence, it will also be demonstrated in
other portions of our work by a process of *analogical*
reasoning that will be still more satisfactory, as it will
be more copious and more definite. It will also be demonstrated by its result in the system of which this
statement constitutes the foundation; a system that
will realize for the first time Philosophy as " the *science*
of things Divine and of things Human," including
Psychology, Theology, and Ontology, made one as
Body, Soul, and Spirit.

This statement is published in advance of the work
for several reasons, besides the urgent request of friends
who have been interested in the progress of our work.
First, the writer wishes to establish *the law* of Tri-
Personality in connection with *the fact* of Tri-Personality in God, as they are here stated, upon internal
ontological evidence alone ; so that he may have a
right to use these as a foundation for the psychological
and theological theories which, together with other
facts now generally recognized, are to be used in illustrating and more completely demonstrating this Law
and this Fact, so that it may not be said that the writer
has *begged* a single question, or assumed any other hypothesis than the original one contained in this statement. He therefore challenges the whole world to
controvert either the premises or the conclusions here
stated, feeling confident that no valid argument can
be brought against them ; external authority being of
course out of the question. He will thus be doubly

armed ; because, as the Law of Tri-Personality is the law according to which, or corresponding with which, all natural things are created ; the mass of *external* evidence that can be brought in support of this statement would be abundantly sufficient even if no other existed.

Another reason for this publication is, that a demonstration of Tri-Personality upon a rational or spiritual basis is particularly needed at the present time ; not only for the purpose of turning the mind from naturalism and materialism, in which it is now immersed, but also for the purpose of redeeming Truth from the bondage of a morbid sentimentalism under whose tyrannical sway it is now suffering a sort of martyrdom ; for, judging from the effect that has been produced by it upon the mind of the writer, it is calculated to produce such a result. Such has been the increase of naturalism in this country, that the doctrine of Tri-Personality has been very extensively abandoned in the Church. So much so that it has been found impossible to obtain a verdict of heresy against a popular divine who has openly declared it to be nothing but *a poetic fiction made necessary by human imperfection.* Now as all the theological doctrines of the Church are dependent for support upon this fact of Tri-Personality in God, or rather upon *her statement* of this fact, its subversion must of course inevitably lead to their overthrow. It would therefore seem that a *rational demonstration* of this fact, heretofore dependent upon sentimental recognition, ought to be acceptable to the Church as presenting a barrier against the tide of heresy that is now setting so strongly against it. Not that *we* imagine this difficulty to be so serious as it undoubtedly appears to them, because we regard these doctrines as *natural substitutes* for spiritual truth that are destined in the natural course of things to decay and death, that they may experience a resurrection to spiritual life *in a rational form;* and thus, that, although the Church and the doctrines of the Church must always remain, when the religious sentiment *in individuals* is not sufficiently strong to compel subjection to it without any other aid, these doctrines will, of course, be given up by them.

There is another and a very different class of individuals belonging to the " *no Church* " party, and known as Transcendentalists, to which such a statement as the one here offered might be of much more importance. Although these individuals have long since passed beyond the point when the doctrines of the Church could be received through sentimental recognition, — and although their position is removed as far as possible from all that relates to a spiritual order of thought and of experience, — still, the fact that they have exhausted all *natural* sources of instruction, makes it necessary that those of a *spiritual* character should be presented to them, and that the steps of these prodigal sons should be directed towards their father's house. Many of these individuals have arrived at the " *great gulf* " which separates the natural from the spiritual ; and, although no broad highway can be constructed across this gulf for the multitude of travellers through this vale of tears, *for these individuals* it has become *imperative* that some bridge should be provided that shall be competent, with the aid of faith, to enable them to " *pass over* " in security. Even now many are watching in darkness upon this perilous shore for the appearance of some star in the East to guide them on their way. Already they cry, " Watchman, what of the night ? Watchman, what of the night ? and the Watchman replieth: The morning cometh and also the night. If ye will inquire, inquire ye."

As both the *necessity* and the *possibility* of obtaining an absolute ground for philosophy, or any other foundation for Theology than the one given to us in the Scriptures and taught by the Church, may be questioned ; we will, as an introduction to this statement, undertake to demonstrate these two facts, and thus answer the two principal objections that will probably be urged against our system, and which, if true, would render the statement here made entirely unnecessary.

Cicero has defined Philosophy to be *" the Science of things Divine and of things Human ; "* and this definition is undeniably correct, because the very nature of philosophy demands rationality, consistency, or oneness ; and, admitting *a relationship to exist* between the Divine and the Human, philosophy cannot be realized without a foundation in absolute law, that will include and govern *both* the Divine and the Human subject. It therefore becomes evident that no philosophy can be true, and so can neither be permanent or extensively useful ; that is not universal in its character, scientific in its form, and founded in absolute law ; or in those universal laws of being in which God exists and through which he manifests himself; so that these laws shall govern all its departments and unite them in one general system. This fact seems to have been very well understood by the ancients, it being undeniably apparent that all the fathers of philosophy have attempted in their systems to obtain a foundation in Absolute Law. They failed of course in these attempts, because, being Pagan, and thus confined to conceptions of the absolute taken from a natural or Unitarian point of view, their systems were necessarily characterized as natural, and so were discordant, uncertain, and unsafe in application, and exceedingly limited in use. As all subsequent systems of philosophy have been constructed either out of materials furnished by these philosophical giants of old, — upon theoretical abstractions, — or upon generalizations of partial natural experiences, — these, too, have failed to realize a universal form of philosophy founded upon the cognition of absolute law. Still, it must be evident that this has always been *the aim* of philosophy, and is essential to its permanency and to its use.

Mr. Field, an English writer of some celebrity, and the author of quite a remarkable work upon the subject of colors, has offered " *a Synopsis of Universal Philosophy*," founded upon the fact, that the whole creation, including, of course, the human soul as its head, is bound together in one vast chain of relationship, which is analogical both in its form and in its function, or use. He says, " As there is nothing known that cannot be resolved into correlative elements, all knowledge consists of relations, and the absolute and the privitive, as extremes, are equally excluded from the sphere of knowledge or philosophy. We hold, therefore, that the universe is, to human cognizance, a universe of relations or analogy, and that all true analogy springs from universal relation ; — that the primary relations of things are invariable and eternal, whence all knowledge is systematic and constant, inasmuch as it partakes of these universal relations or first principles ; — and, therefore, that all certainty is certainty of relation only, and not absolute, for of the absolute we have only indication, but not knowledge, or comprehension."

Now this is very well so far as it recognizes an important fact in the phenomena of existence, which is that of universal relationship. But Mr. Field has committed a capital error that is fatal to his theory in excluding the consideration of absolute Being, which is the *basis* of this relationship, — and in supposing that *a science of relations* could be constructed by *generalizing the facts of observation and experience, and in tracing the relationships of use in the phenomena of nature.* As nature is not harmonious, but *contains an element of opposition, and so of discord,* which is the rock upon which all other systems have foundered, a universal system of philosophy could not possibly be produced by such a method. The study and classification of natural phenomena cannot help us to *understand* them, because *the support of this chain and the key by which only it can be unlocked are to be found nowhere but in God.* A knowledge of the relationship existing between the Absolute and the Phenomenal, or between the Spiritual and the Natural, is the very key to the whole mystery of life ; and this relationship cannot of course be discovered until we know what the Absolute, or the Spiritual, really is. As the ground of all natural phenomena, and of all natural law, is the Absolute, it must of course follow that it is only so far as we obtain some adequate conception of this absolute ground that we can obtain any

2

principle of classification or of analysis that can lead us *in the direction* of truth. In other words, as God is the sole ground and cause of all existence, and as all things are for this reason created in his likeness, so that, to use the language of Scripture, "*the invisible things of God from the creation of the World are clearly seen, being understood by the things that are made, even his eternal power and godhead,*" a correct conception of *the modes of his existence and activity* must of course be the only legitimate ground of philosophy.

This may be illustrated by the fact that the *religious instinct* through which we obtain a recognition of the statements contained in the Scriptures and made by the Church of these identical spiritual facts, is the ruling power of the natural mind, and the highest point of natural contemplation ; so that even in the natural, Theology becomes the life of Philosophy. It is thus a well known fact that the philosophy of a people is always determined by their theology ; that is, by their conceptions of the nature of a first cause. In proportion as this theology is in harmony with the Spiritual, or representative of spiritual ideas, GOD is regarded as the ground of existence, and his nature is interrogated for an explanation of the phenomena of life ; and in proportion as this theology is natural, MATTER is regarded as the ground of existence, and the physical laws which govern its development are interrogated for an explanation of the phenomena of life. Hence the numerous material theories of modern times growing out of the natural unitarian tendency of the age. Even transcendentalism tends to sensualism, and etherialism tends to materialism, as the self-styled spiritual philosophies of the present day show; some of which have undertaken to trace back the human soul through animal and vegetable *into a mineral substance,* from which they assume that the soul became developed in accordance with the laws of physical growth. It is true that the religious instinct only determines *the character* of philosophy and *can never furnish a foundation for any system,* for the reason that it is not *intellectual,* but *sentimental,* and so of the nature of *affection ;* and thus, although it is able to recognize in an apprehensive manner things that are *representative* of spiritual ideas and relationships when these are presented to it, it is not competent to furnish any foundation even for a philosophic statement ; but is dependent upon natural experiences and natural thought for the statement and illustration of its ideas. These are of course discordant and *anti-*philosophical, because Nature, being governed by the principle of *diversity,* can never be anything else. The Church, therefore, has never had any philosophy. It has never depended upon *intellectual,* but always upon *sentimental* recognition ; and has never adopted the Spiritual Ideas which are embodied in its theological systems as the *foundation* for truth, or for philosophy, but have regarded these as a *superstructure* of truth that was to be supported by anything that seemed to answer the purpose. All the Pagan philosophies, even the Epicurean, were, therefore, made use of by the fathers of the Church, as I shall presently show, in defending and inculcating its peculiar views ; although these, being Unitarian, must be in substance *opposite* to Christianity. These facts are sufficient to show how much necessity there is for some statement of *absolute ontological* truth that shall serve as a foundation both for Psychology and Theology, so that Philosophy, by embracing psychological, theological, and ontological truth as Body, Soul, and Spirit, shall furnish a universal form by which truth shall be redeemed from diversity and discord, and become harmoniously one as *"the Science of things Divine and of things Human."* That Philosophy *demands* an absolute basis, then, is not to be doubted. The only question to be settled is, has it here been realized? This will be settled first, by the *self-evident* character of the foundation that will here be laid; next by the *analogical proof* that will be furnished from every department of knowledge; and, lastly, by *the results* of its application in explaining the phenomena of revelation, of observation, and of the consciousness, and in realizing satisfactory systems of psychology and theology.

The other objection to this system, that it pretends to offer a foundation for Christian Theology different from the one given to us in the Scriptures as interpreted by the Church, will probably be considered by the men of the Church as the most serious objection of the two. If the system should really pretend to offer anything as a foundation for theology, *that is not contained in or sanctioned by the Scriptures*, it would indeed be a serious objection. Such, however, is not the fact, as the theology here to be presented will be in every particular supported by quotations from the Scriptures, and the corner-stone of our whole system may be found included in two quotations from Romans and Ecclesiasticus, given at the commencement of our chapter upon the Laws of Correspondence, although no one has probably ever before seen them in this light. Indeed our theology will be found to be *essentially* the same, or the same, *in substance*, as that of the Church, although as to *its form*, being internal, spiritual, and rational, instead of being external, natural, and discordant, it will be found in every respect different. Still these men of the Church may possibly object to it upon the ground that, as the theology of the Bible belongs to a spiritual order of thought that is opposite to a natural order, and is thus separated from and opposed to the natural understanding, no other evidence than the testimony of the Scriptures as interpreted by the Church *can ever* be obtained for it, the Bible being the only revelation of spiritual truth that can ever be made to mankind, and the Church being its only authorized interpreter ; for although the claim to *a private interpretation* of the Scriptures was necessarily set up by Protestantism to secure a separation from Romanism, no Church can tolerate a departure from its creed, or recognize any other interpreter of the Bible than itself.

There could not, however, be anything more indefensible than a position like this, because it is an undeniable philosophical fact that will be demonstrated in a thousand ways in the course of this work, that all existence and all consciousness, as well as all belief, is a result produced by the union of external facts with internal principles ; this being demanded by a universal law of being ; so that no revelation can possibly be made to the mind *from without* except as it *corresponds with a revelation made to it from within*. Admitting, as we do, not only that the Bible *contains* a revelation of

Divine Truth, but that *it is* a revelation of Divine Truth, even the letter of which is divinely inspired, — and this is more than most of those who belong to the Church would be willing to do, — the question comes up, *How is this Divine Revelation to be communicated to the mind ?* or, *By what principle of the mind is it to be interpreted ?* For although the presentation and exposition of the Scriptures may be *the first condition,* they can never be *the cause* of their recognition and reception, it being impossible that what is external to the mind, and must, therefore, be made known to it through sensation, should ever be anything more to it than *suggestive,* that something *in the mind* may be furnished with *material for production and be excited to incarnate itself in form.* There are two modes in which the spiritual truths contained in the Scriptures are recognized and appropriated by the mind. The first mode is by a natural sentimental recognition, as interpreted by individual natural experiences, and stated in the forms of the natural understanding. This recognition and statement are made *possible* because the Scriptures contain a *natural letter* that is correspondent to natural thought and natural experiences, while at the same time this natural letter is *representative of spiritual ideas.* The second mode in which Spiritual Truth is made known to the mind is by *an intuition of the Laws of Being,* by the application of which Christian Theology is realized as *a Science,* and all natural as well as all spiritual phenomena are explained, and their true relationships disclosed to the mind ; for although this intuition of absolute law could not be realized without the intervention of an external suggestive principle, which is provided for us in the Scriptures, — *being realized*, all the spiritual phenomena of which the theology of the Church is only the discordant natural representative, must be at once *reproduced* by it, and the representative character of all natural things revealed.

Now it is *the first* of these modes that has heretofore exclusively prevailed in the Church ; and this may be known because the beliefs of the Church are apprehensive, affectional, and poetical, instead of being comprehensive, rational, and philosophical, — because they do not recognize spiritual or absolute *Law*, but only take cognizance of spiritual *Phenomena*, — because they are connected with external natural thought and the most external natural experiences, — and because they are found in the greatest diversity and discord, while the spiritual must of course include Universality, Unity, and Harmony. If no other recognition of spiritual truth than this of the Church were possible, its promulgation would be nothing but a mockery, because, as " *spiritual things must be spiritually discerned,*" and thus can only be recognized by *a spiritual faculty*, this truth could never *really* be recognized, or received and appropriated, by man, and so could be of no possible use to him, but, on the contrary, must seem to be a cruelly unnecessary source of unhappiness. It is therefore, that as the religious sentiment, upon which this recognition of the Church depends for its support, loses its influence over the mind, the dogmas of the Church are at once rejected as something abhorrent to its thought, and repugnant to its feeling, and come to be regarded as an incubus of superstition that it is the greatest relief to be rid of.

As this sentimental recognition, then, has failed to give to Theology that rationality, universality, permanency, and use, that a form of spiritual or absolute truth must evidently be calculated to afford, it must be evident that we are to look to *some other source* for the realization of a theology that, being founded in the intuition of *absolute law,* shall combine these requisites. That the realization of such a theology is now the great desideratum, cannot, we think, be questioned; and to doubt the possibility of its accomplishment, would be the greatest impiety, madness, and folly. It is true that the Church, with all her diversities and discords, can never be dispensed with, because she performs *a great preparatory service* in providing materials in the natural, representative and suggestive of the spiritual, and out of which the spiritual itself must be born, so that she may be said to be *the mother of Christianity.* But although it is *through* the Church, it is only *by the overshadowing of the Spirit,* that this birth becomes possible.

It is also true, as the Church affirms, that the Scriptures, being a record of spiritual truth, cannot be comprehended, or even recognized by the natural understanding, which is opposite or antagonistic; and we therefore willingly admit that, *so long as this understanding is the only test of truth,* and *the only interpreter of the Scriptures,* this *interpretation* should be left exclusively to those who have been fitted for such a task by a long and profound study of these records and of the traditions and decisions of the Church; and that this *recognition* should be left exclusively to a sentimental apprehension that has no reference to human thought,

feeling, or ideas of consistency. It is therefore that
the Church of Rome wisely discourages the reading of
the Scriptures unaccompanied by her own interpretations ; for in undertaking to rationalize, or to comprehend, the Bible with no better light than that of the
natural understanding, we shall certainly succeed in
nothing but in destroying all its spiritual character, and
in turning its waters of life into a deadly poison. It
cannot be true, however, that man is always to be confined to this inferior kind of intellectual consciousness.
It can be clearly shown that this is nothing but a
reflection, or rather a *refraction*, from some higher
source of intelligence that makes a part of his nature,
and without which he could not possess even this,
although no other evidence may have appeared of its
existence than the humanitarian character that it has
imparted to the lower powers of the mind. The command given to man, in the Scriptures, that he should
" *Love God with his whole heart*," is a perfect assurance
of this fact ; for, were not man endowed with *a capacity
for knowing God*, which must of course be a capacity
for absolute knowledge, or for the cognition of absolute
law, this command would be so great an absurdity as
to be perfectly ludicrous. If man were not so endowed
he certainly could never *know* anything of God, and so
could never *love* him. All that man could ever love
would be some image of his own creation ; and this he
could not of course love with his whole heart, but only
so far as he supposed it to minister to some selfish
gratification. All this being as clearly demonstrable
as any proposition in Euclid, I would not merely *suggest
as a possibility*, but would *affirm as a necessary fact*, that,

3

— besides a *Natural Understanding,* that is adapted to
the comprehension of truths belonging to a *natural order,*
— and besides a *Sentimental Nature,* that is adapted to
a discordant apprehensive recognition, through sensible
images and natural modes of thought and of experience as various as the condition of the subject, of
truths belonging to a spiritual order, — man has been
endowed with *Reason,* or with a rational principle that
may be designated as *a Spiritual Understanding,* — that
this is adapted to the comprehension of truths belonging to *a spiritual order,* — and that these must be susceptible of a rational, scientific, or truly philosophic
statement, because it is only through such a statement
that *anything* can be comprehended or really known,
and because Spirituality and Rationality are inseparable. This idea of a Spiritual Understanding through
which man becomes competent to realize a true conception of God, or of the modes of his existence and manifestation, and thus is able to attain to the knowledge
of Absolute Law, is not by any means a vague idea in
the mind of the writer, but one that has been developed
into scientific thought. This spiritual nature of man,
which consists of three principles, corresponding with
Truth, Good, and Beauty, will be analyzed and described in the psychological portion of our work as
THE REASON. It will there be shown how it is that
this confers upon man *humanity,* gives to his understanding the form of *rationality,* and to the will *self-
consciousness,* and *makes possible* to him that sentimental
recognition of spiritual phenomena which we designate
as *religious experience;* so that if he were deprived of

this source of absolute knowledge he could be nothing more than a higher kind of animal.

Such being the effects that are produced even by the unconscious presence of this spiritual principle, when only manifesting itself *remotely* through lower natural mediums, we shall be able to form some idea of what its potency and power will be when its manifestations shall be *direct*, and furnish a medium for the communication to the soul of that wisdom which is "the brightness of the everlasting light, the unspotted mirror of the power of God, and the image of his goodness. *Being but one, she can do all things :* and remaining in herself she maketh all things new : and in all ages entering into holy souls, she maketh them friends of God, and prophets." *

* Wisdom of Solomon.

THE LAW

OF

TRI-PERSONALITY.

PRELIMINARY STATEMENT.

IN constructing systems of philosophy it is customary, as it is of course necessary, to commence with some conception of *the Cause* of existence from which a statement of *the Laws* of existence can be deduced or evolved ; it being manifestly impossible that we should be able to understand or to explain *an Effect* without first understanding something of *the Cause* by which it is produced ; and to call that *Philosophy* which is not founded upon a System of Laws, by which it is pervaded, and made one, and to which all its statements are referable, would be manifestly absurd. It is therefore that Philosophy has been defined to be "the *Science* of things *Divine* and of things *Human* ;" although no one has yet succeeded in obtaining such a conception of God, and in framing from this such a system of laws as shall include *both* the things which are Divine and the things which are Human ; and thus it has not been possible that *either* should have been understood, or that

Philosophy should have been realized as legitimate Science, or as a System of Absolute Truth.

All philosophies heretofore constructed have been founded either upon the Law of Unity, the Law of Duality, or Diversity, or from an incongruous mixture and discordant application of these two opposite principles. No philosophy now known has succeeded in realizing the *Marriage*, or union as one, of these two principles or laws, because this union is possible only through the *Law of Trinity*, which has never yet been applied as a law in philosophy, or been stated as a productive philosophic principle.

Three principles operating as one, and stated or included in the formula of Wisdom, Love, and Power, — or Intellect, Affection, and Will, — these being related as Body, Soul, and Spirit, — have often been recognized both as the cause and as the universal condition of existence ; and have been very extensively adopted as a basis both for Theology and for Philosophy. As this may be seen to constitute the form of all things, both natural and spiritual, and so is to be regarded as the Law of Unity, or Individuality, we cannot help accepting this idea as a universal law of Being.

We cannot, however, take this *alone* as a guide in our search after Truth, or as the foundation for any system, because it is simply a principle of *generalization* that excludes the possibility of *analysis*, — because it supposes a oneness, or a harmony of parts, that contradicts all experience, so that nothing can be explained by it, — and because, as it must individualize the universe by reducing everything to a simple Infinite Personality in God, instead of *explaining anything*, it would lead to the dissipation or *destruction of everything*, by resolving everything either into Spirit or into Matter. By taking this idea for our guide, we should be led through all the devious mazes of Unitarianism, until, having exhausted all its expedients to obtain a foundation for our belief, or an explanation of our life, we should find that we had succeeded only in realizing *Nihilism*.

Two principles existing in perfect *antagonism*, have sometimes been recognized both as the cause and as the universal condition of existence, and have also been adopted as the foundation both of Theology and Philosophy. As such an antagonism may be seen to exist universally in Nature, and is, indeed, generally acknowledged so to exist, — and as such an opposition supposes a similar opposition in the sources from which natural existence is derived, — we cannot but accept *Dualism*, also, as a universal law of Being. We cannot take this, however, as a guide, or as the foundation for any system, because, although the Law of Duality might enable us to *account for* many of the phenomena of natural life, it would not help us to *explain* them with any satisfaction. Should we take this as our point of departure, as a substitute for the Law of Unity, we should be led into a two-sided contemplation of truth

4

that would be as adverse to the repose of Faith, as to the consistency of Philosophy. By substituting *natural appearances* for *spiritual facts*, we should produce as much confusion, diversity, and uncertainty in our philosophical conclusions, as in our religious belief; and by demanding the recognition of two independent spiritual principles existing in perpetual hostility, we should reproduce all the monstrosities of the grossest Heathen superstition.

It would seem, then, that, although the laws of Unity and Duality, — upon one or the other of which, or upon the incongruous mixture of which, all philosophies have heretofore been founded, — are legitimate Laws of Being, and thus are *both* to be in some way recognized; it must be evident that neither of these can be sufficient as the foundation of a system capable of satisfying the Reason, of explaining the phenomena of life, or of serving as the exponent of Spirituality or Christianity; while the combination of them would be fatal to all consistency, and thus fatal to all true philosophy. We will, therefore, while adopting them both as *elements* in Truth, or as laws of the Reason, go one step further, and add to these another element, which is the *Law of Trinity*. By the application, or by the *addition* of this law, which will hereafter be stated and explained, we shall find that Unity and Duality, although perfectly opposite, will become completely reconciled, and by union with it constitute a living and productive principle capable of furnishing a foundation that shall be adequate to the support of a universal system of Truth. We will take, then, for our point of departure, the Law of Unity, the Law of Duality, and the Law of Trinity, as a three-fold form of Absolute Truth, which we may designate as the *Trinitarian Principle*, or LAW OF TRI-PERSONALITY; recognizing in these three elements the same relation of Body, Soul, and Spirit that has already been recognized in the elements composing the Law of Unity or Individuality, which are Wisdom, Love, and Power; and the same necessity that Body and Soul should become one, in order that Spirit, as the highest personality, should be realized. We will first make a statement of these three Laws as scientific formulas, and make an application of these formulas in obtaining a conception of the three-fold form in which God exists as Father, Son, and Holy Ghost, three persons, but one God. We will next expand these into more definite thought by illustration, and apply them as principles of classification and analysis, in the explanation and comprehension of all things relating to the nature and destiny of the Soul; in doing which we shall realize Philosophy in its absolute character as " the Science of things Divine and of things Human," including the elements of Psychology, Theology, and Ontology, made one as Body, Soul, and Spirit.

LAW OF UNITY.

As the condition of *Being*, everything must exist as a simple Individuality, which becomes realized by the union of an intellectual and an affectional principle combined and operating as one, and therefore embracing a three-fold function of Intellect, Affection, and Activity,— or Wisdom, Love, and Power, — as Body, Soul, and Spirit.

LAW OF DUALITY.

As the condition of *Production*, all things must exist *in pairs*, as Male and Female; the first being characterized as *Intellectual*, and the second as *Affectional;* and also in pairs as Masculine and Feminine, the first being characterized as *Internal*, and the second as *External;* which Dualities must *originally* exist under a double or complex law of *affinity* and *antipathy*, and so include the principles of *mutual attraction* and *mutual opposition.*

LAW OF TRINITY.

As the condition of *Absolute Life*, and thus of permanency, or perpetuity, all things must become one with Absolute Unity by the *Marriage of Opposites* produced

by the sacrifice of Individualism, or Self-ism ; and recognizing Infinite Wisdom and Infinite Love as the Life
of all things, become a three-fold Personality existing
in three several spheres of consciousness, made one as
Body, Soul, and Spirit.

UNITY,

THE LAW OF INDIVIDUALITY.

ACCORDING to our statement of the Law of Unity, as the condition of Being, or of Existence, everything must exist as a simple Individuality ; which becomes realized by the union of an intellective with an affective principle combined and operating as one, and thus embracing a three-fold function of Intellect, Affection, and Activity, — or Wisdom, Love, and Power, — as Body, Soul, and Spirit.

The first question, therefore, that arises is, how is this Idea, or this Law, to be applied in obtaining a conception of God ? for this, as well as the laws of Duality and Trinity, if true, must be found to originate in the constitution of God, from whom all things are derived, and a correct conception of which constitution must be obtained, before we can commence the construction of any permanent system of truth.

If we apply this Law of Individuality to God, as a
simple and not as a complex Being, we realize Unitarianism, or Pantheism ; which appears in three several
aspects, according to the manner in which this law is
applied.   If we regard him as purely *Spiritual,* we
realize the universe as a *spiritual emanation,* and regard
all the appearances of Matter as deceptive, — as in the
theory of Berkley.   If we regard him as purely *Material,* we realize the Universe as a *material development,*
and regard all the conceptions of Spiritual Existence as
fallacious, — as in the Epicurean Philosophy.   If we regard him as *compounded* of Spirit and Matter, which are
originally one in essence, and related as Soul and Body,
we realize the Universe as a creation by God, from and
in Himself, or as God developing, or externalizing Himself in the Universe, — as in the Ionic, Pythagorean,
Stoic, and other systems.

The last of these conceptions being the most congenial with the complex nature of the human mind,
has been most generally adopted as the foundation of
Philosophy ; for although many systems have recognized a sort of dualism, or antagonism between Spirit
and Matter, they have generally recognized Matter as
originating in and *emanating from* an Infinite Spiritual
source ; and have, probably for the sake of practicability,
although at the expense of rationality, regarded its opposition or imperfection as occasioned by the *greater or
less distance* which separates it from this source, towards

which it is constantly progressing in its return. By far the greater number of systems, however, have adopted the more consistent and directly Unitarian theory ; and applied the Law of Unity to Spirit and Matter ; by which they become *individualized,* and all things are resolved into one sphere, as harmonious, or homogeneous, — Spirit being regarded as *Active,* — Matter as *harmoniously Passive,* — and their union as *Productive.*

Now Spirit and Matter are so associated in our minds with the idea of antagonism, and the belief in Matter is so much more *natural* than a belief in Spirit, that there is a constant tendency in Pantheism to *Materialism,* and but for the influence of the Religious sentiment, this would be irresistible. It was, probably, the recognition of this fatal Atheistic tendency, which clings to every philosophy in which Matter is recognized, that led the pious Bishop Berkley to construct that remarkable argument which *demonstrates,* from a spiritual point of view, the *non-existence of a Material Universe ;* a conclusion that is equally Pantheistic, and as much to be deprecated, as that of the Materialist, or Atheist. It is thus that Unitarianism must always be destructive ; and end either in the deification of Matter and death of the Soul, or in the destruction of Matter and thus of all individuality in existence ; which will amount to the same thing.

We cannot accept Unitarianism, then, because it is anti-philosophical, — anti-spiritual, — and anti-produc-

5

tive, or destructive. It is anti-philosophical, because, although all the *forms* of things, when considered *individually*, will be found to correspond with this Law of Unity, — as the *substance*, the *relations*, and thus the *manifestations* of things are evidently governed by an *opposite Law that is dualistic*, the principle of Unitarianism is found to be utterly incompetent to explain the phenomena of life, or the great facts of existence. It is anti-spiritual, because it does not recognize the positive antagonism that exists between the natural and the spiritual, and the necessity for self-sacrifice ; which are the great ideas of Spirituality or Christianity. It is anti-productive, or destructive, because it demands the destruction either of Spirit or of Matter, without *the union* of which the universe cannot be made to subsist ; and because in opposing Spiritualism it must eventually destroy itself, or rather be destroyed by it.

In order that we may obtain a clearer idea of the nature of Unitarianism, I will present a short analysis of this sect in Philosophy and the Church, and point out the tendency that it has to cause the destruction, or dissipation of all existence. That it must eventually lead to the destruction of the individual who refuses to abandon it, has been recognized in all Christian Theology, and will be demonstrated in the System of Theology here to be given.

Unitarianism, as its name denotes, is founded in the idea that everything emanates from, and is resolvable into, *one essence*, or substance, and is thus included in one sphere ; being opposite to the idea in which Trinitarianism is founded, which is, that all things emanated from, and are resolvable into, *two opposite essences*, or substances, to one of which *Heaven* is the sphere or habitation, and to the other, *Hell.* Unitarianism might, therefore, be defined to be *the belief in one principle or substance ;* and all the opinions peculiar to it may be seen to grow out of, and to be referable to, this particular belief. In its *manifestation*, however, although always essentially Pantheistic, as the above definition implies, it becomes divided, in accordance with the universal law of production just stated, into *Idealism*, or *Pantheism*, and *Realism*, or *Naturalism*, as this manifestation is Intellectual or Affectional, having reference to Truth or to God ; while *both* become again divided as they partake of an *internal* or an *external* character. Thus we find that Pantheism, as the exponent of Truth, sometimes takes the form of *Spiritualism*, and attempts to refer everything to the operation of forces or laws which are modes of Infinite Activity, by which all existence becomes dissipated, and all individuality destroyed ; and sometimes takes the form of *Materialism*, and attempts to resolve everything into a succession of physical phenomena, which become *developed* according to laws inherent in material substance ; ascending in series from mineral to vegetable, from vegetable to animal, and

from animal to human life, by which both Spirituality
and Immortality are destroyed.

Thus also we find that Naturalism, as the exponent
of Good, sometimes takes the form of *Transcendentalism*,
judging of everything by *the motive*, and demanding the
internal development of the individual, by securing to
him the free exercise of his affectional or passional
nature, because this must lead him to the realization of
Good in its highest form as an internal governing principle, — and sometimes takes the form of *Moralism*, judging of everything by *the appearance*, and demanding an
external government for the individual that shall be in
accordance with some *generally accepted standard* of use
or good.

Although all Unitarian systems of thought, however,
must be characterized either as Spiritual Pantheism, as
Material Pantheism, as Transcendentalism, or as Moralism, — and although all these forms of Unitarianism are
perfectly hostile or antagonistic, — they are seldom, if
ever, found except in *discordant combination*. This is
because the human mind, as a natural production, exists
in diversity and discord both intellectually and affectionally, and thus cannot be satisfied except in the
recognition of things which are also in diversity and
discord. It is thus kept in perpetual agitation and conflict, and although Reason, as the spiritual principle in
man, is continually demanding *consistency*, or *repose* for
the mind, this can never be realized except by a

universal philosophy founded upon absolute cognition, or by that final *rest in God* consequent upon its union with him in spiritual life, which is *the Sabbath* of the Soul.

Pantheism is the most philosophical or rational aspect of Unitarianism, because, being the exponent of truth, its province is to discover and to establish *natural law,* and it is thus impressed with the necessity of *theoretical consistency.* Denying, as it must, the existence of evil as a positive principle, it regards all *appearances of evil* as nothing but the *imperfection of good,* as shade or darkness is supposed to be the imperfection, or obstruction of light, being *an incident of natural growth,* and essential to the development and education of the soul. Thus one of their own poets has said,

> " For out of woe, and out of crime,
> Draws the soul a lore sublime."

And the same writer has asserted that the soul, whether in the brothel or on the gallows, is constantly ascending towards perfection. The necessity of human actions, is also a doctrine of Pantheism. It denies that freedom can ever exist for man because he must always be bounded by the ever revolving circle of nature, and included in an everlasting chain of causes and consequences. Looking, as it does, from a natural point of view, it cannot without a violation of consistency avoid coming to this conclusion. Much valuable truth, therefore, is to be learned from it that cannot be derived from any other natural source; for that everything is really good, because designed by an Infinite wisdom and love for the production of the greatest ultimate good to each individual, is a truth to which the Church *has never attained ;* and the idea of *necessity* is one that it has never been able to retain for any length of time, although it is so indispensable in the construction of all Christian as well as of all Pagan Theology.   Although a necessary *element* in truth, however, it is well known that the tendency of Pantheism is *Atheistic,* and leads to the destruction of all existence, either by the dissipation of matter, and with this all individuality, or by the *establishment* of individuality and the dissipation of all *spiritual life,* and thus of all immortality.

Naturalism is the most unphilosophical, or irrational aspect of Unitarianism, because, being the exponent of Good, its province is to discover and to establish *natural use,* which is external or phenomenal; and the more external or superficial the mind becomes, the more discordant it is.   Both in its internal and its external aspects it is confined to the observation of *natural phenomena,* — accepts only those ideas which can be confined within natural forms of thought, — and believes only in what is *apparent,* supposing this to be the only reality.   Both internalists and externalists, therefore, believe in a self-determining power of the will, that always decides it to this or to that action as it shall choose and *because it chooses*, and thus *disclaim the operation of motives ;* this being a belief in that deceptive fact of the natural consciousness which is recognized by Lord Kames and other philosophers as "*the delusive sense of liberty.*" This is because the idea of Free-Will, or human free agency, is a fact of natural consciousness observable internally by the former, as well as an apparent fact of natural life observable externally by the latter.

The two elements contained in Naturalism, however, which are Transcendentalism and Moralism, are *relatively* consistent and inconsistent, because they are relatively internal and external ; and the internal is allied both to simplicity and rationality *in the life*, while the external is allied to duplicity and inconsistency, or discord. It will therefore be found that there is in many respects a perfect *antagonism* between these two exponents of natural good. While the former demands that the internal and the external shall become one, or that the external manifestation shall correspond with the internal life, the latter demands concealment for the one and a false appearance for the other. It is true that it is only for *good*, of which it is the highest exponent, that Transcendentalism demands consistency ; because here, Good is elevated above Truth, which, therefore, is either sacrificed for it or kept in subjection to it. *Theoretical* consistency is thus regarded by Transcendentalists with the greatest contempt. It is

also true that an external or *apparent* consistency is
demanded by Moralism, because it requires an external
conformity to some arbitrary standard of good ; but
this does not affect the position here taken because the
consistency of Transcendentalism is *real,* while that of
Moralism is *fictitious,* and even in this, the opposition
between these two elements of Naturalism is apparent.   Let us attend for a moment to some of these
differences.

Transcendentalists, as internalists, relying upon an
internal direction, become observers of the phenomena of
the consciousness, which include the *motives* or *causes* of
action ; while the Moralists, as externalists, relying upon an *external direction,* become observers of the phenomena of *life,* which include *the consequences* of action.
The first, although avoiding those metaphysical abstractions to which the Pantheist is devoted as *the Law of
Truth,* are quite as devoted in the search after and
application of what they consider to be *the Law of Good ;*
while the second, eschewing all principles, confine themselves exclusively to *practical results,* and the application
of external rules of conduct established by authority.
The first, being impressed with the mistaken notions
that the Law of Good should be *supreme,* and that the
moral sense is in every one competent to *furnish* this
Law,— not understanding that in the natural everything
is *relative* and nothing *positive,* so that the law of good
is brought into *diversity* and cannot possibly be made

one, or rendered universally applicable ; — become strenuous for the application of those feelings and principles which govern *their own conduct,* and which they feel to be the law of right for *themselves,* to all the fluctuating and unequal conditions and circumstances of social life both by themselves *and others ;* not considering that, if the Law of Good is the supreme principle, *the female* should also be supreme, and that they should, to be consistent, submit themselves to *female rule.* By thus insisting upon the *universal* application of these *partial* principles of use, without having any regard for the consequences of such application, they run into all kinds of fanaticism, and produce all kinds of mischief.

The second, on the other hand, — although not denying the capacity of the moral sense to *perceive* what is right, because this, as an *apparent fact,* is recognized by both, — being impressed with the idea that the Will is not sufficiently strong to compel *obedience* to this law of right, but that it is, *in the masses,* overcome by an opposite tendency, distrust and repudiate all independent individual action ; and, being governed by expediency, and regarding *nothing but* consequences, require the obedience of all to some established external authority that shall decide for all what is right. By thus insisting upon the suppression of all individual activity, — the realization of immediate and apparent external use, — and the establishment of some arbitrary external

6

authority,—— they debase *the standard* of morals, and throw an insuperable obstacle in the way of all progress and of all improvement.

Again, the first deny that any tendency to evil exists in the nature of man, and assert that all abuses are the result of a false organization of society and an unhealthy condition of the public sentiment; while the second admit that a tendency to evil as well as to good exists in the nature of man, and assert that the influence of society, or of the public sentiment, is calculated, and is necessary, to check the one and to encourage the other. This is because the first derive their opinions from the observation of *internal phenomena* as presented to the consciousness, that will not readily acknowledge the presence of *an evil motive*, and because they are too consistent to admit the idea that a natural tendency to evil can exist in a being who is *an emanation from God in whom it never existed ;* —— while the second derive their opinions from the observation of *external phenomena* which present the appearance of mingled good and evil, and from the fact that man *appears* to know the one, while, when unrestrained by the law or public opinion he practices the other.

Moralists do not, of course, believe in the *absolute antagonism* between good and evil as recognized by the Church, or, indeed, entertain any speculations with regard to the abstract nature of these qualities. *The measure* of good is with them *use*, and its reward and

consequence *happiness ;* while the measure of evil is
with them *abuse,* and its punishment and consequence
unhappiness ; while *the regulation* of this measure belongs to the Church, to the laws, and to the public
sentiment, which are generally harmonious. It is true
that they appear to regard the moral sense as capable
of furnishing the law of Good, and as *constituting the
Spiritual Principle in man ;* and regard evil as originating in certain animal appetites and selfish propensi-
ties which they suppose to be *".the lusts of the flesh "*
alluded to in the Scriptures, *the letter* of which, so far
as it can be made to harmonize with their peculiar
views, they *patronize,* or adopt as an additional support ;
while they suppose that the regeneration and salvation
of the individual is effected by the subjection of these
to the spiritual law of conscience through the operation
of free-will. Now this, one would think, was sufficiently
external. Even this, however, is more theoretical than
practical, is more apparent than real, because they have
never been able to define in what this moral nature consists, but *take for granted* that this and the prevailing
public sentiment is one and the same thing ; while
regeneration with them means *culture,* and salvation
means *an increase of happiness ;* for salvation and damnation in the *theological sense* of these terms are regarded by them as the offspring of a horrible superstition.
With regard to *the nature* of the reward and the punishment that is supposed by them to attend the observance

and the violation of these moral conditions, or this arbitrary code of moral obligation, considerable diversity of opinion prevails among them.   Some believe that punishment is *arbitrary*, and is inflicted *from without* as a *penalty*, — some that it is *necessary*, and is inflicted *from within* as a *discipline* ; — and others believe that the soul is, by the condition of its nature, made subject to certain moral laws that have been promulgated by God as a universal regulator to the thoughts, the feelings, and the actions of man, — laws which are as unerring in their operation in inflicting punishments and in conferring rewards as those which appear to us to govern the *physical* world.   Hence, they conclude that it is of the greatest importance that every one should make himself acquainted with these moral laws by attending to instruction from the prescribed sources, because, as in physics, the unconscious violation of these laws through ignorance must be quite as fatal as the conscious violation of them against knowledge.   These diversities, however, are too numerous to mention, and the further enumeration of them here is unnecessary ; for as both Transcendentalism and Moralism belong to the sphere of life or of experience, they will both be carefully analyzed and described in making our statement of "*the Laws of Succession*" as applied to the development of human nature.

So long as man is confined to an external sphere of consciousness, the tendency of Naturalism to self-worship and self-destruction does not distinctly appear, because he is at this time more or less under subjection to Society and to the Church, — acknowledges the validity of some truths belonging to a spiritual order, — and thus inconsistently maintains opinions which are mutually destructive. But when he begins to be *a reality* by the realization of an internal sphere of consciousness, so that *the individual himself* can become manifested, — when he demands consistency for his life, and the realization of *his own* highest ideas or conceptions of truth and of good, as *the higher Law* which should supersede all others and *govern* all others as well as himself ; — and finally, when he becomes *a worshipper of natural perfection,* or of the true and the good in the beautiful, — for to this point Unitarianism must necessarily come, — then the impious and suicidal tendency of Naturalism becomes apparent, as it stretches forth its hand to seize the sceptre of God ; for now, as it happened from the first coming of John to the first coming of Christ, as recorded by St. Matthew,* *" the kingdom of heaven suffereth violence, and the violent take it by force."* This must be apparent if we reflect. We have seen that Unitarianism rests upon the ground that God exists as *a simple individuality,* or as the one Infinite Life, — and that Nature is thus either *an emanation from him,* or *a creation in him,* it can make no difference

---

* St. Matthew, 11 : 12.

which ; — for, should it, for an instant, admit the idea that the Universe was created out of something *separate from God*, the further admission must, to the rational mind, *inevitably follow*, that *this something* is by necessity *opposite, or opposed, to God;* and this would bring in at once the fact of *positive or absolute evil existing as the life of nature*, and in its train all those peculiar doctrines of the Church which it has always been its great object to oppose and to overthrow. The idea that *Nature is a part of God*, being *necessarily incidental to Unitarianism*, it follows, as a matter of course, that Unitarianism when it comes to be consistent, must embrace the worship of Nature as God, or the worship of God in Nature, which is the same thing, and thus must embrace self-worship because man is *" the Lord of Nature."* We therefore find as a final result man setting up his claim to an *infinite personality*, and to an *infinite scope to his activity* unrestrained by any law whatever ; so that this is not a mere theory, but may be seen in actual manifestation, as I shall presently have occasion to show.

It will be understood, of course, that we are considering Unitarianism from an abstract spiritual point of view, and not from a practical one. The *full development* of this principle, of which we have here given a slight sketch, but all for which we now have room, is indispensable to the progress or development of the soul, and no single phase of it could possibly be dispensed with. In a *spiritual condition* of the soul, however, or after it has entered into a spiritual sphere of consciousness, a *continuance* of the self-worship and denial of Divine Truth which it includes, must inevitably lead to its destruction. It is therefore that the prophet Isaiah in denouncing from a spiritual position those who shall become guilty of this unpardonable sin says : ——

" For behold, the Lord will come with fire, and with his chariots like a whirlwind ; to render his anger with fury and his rebuke with flames of fire. For by fire and by his sword will the Lord plead with all flesh, and the slain of the Lord shall be many. They that sanctify themselves and purify themselves in the gardens *behind one tree in the midst,* eating swine's flesh, and the abomination, and the field mouse, shall be consumed together saith the Lord."

" For the Lord will have mercy on Jacob, and will yet choose Israel and set them in their own land : and the stranger shall be joined with thee, and they will cleave to the house of Jacob. And it shall come to pass, that thou shall take up this proverb against the King of Babylon and say, How hath the oppressor ceased ! the golden city ceased ! Thy pomp is brought down to the grave, and the noise of thy viols : the worm is spread under thee, and the worms cover thee. For thou hast said in thine heart, I will ascend unto heaven, I will exalt my throne above the stars of God.

I will ascend above the height of the clouds : I will be like the most High. Yet thou shalt be brought down to Hell, to the sides of the pit."

In stating the difference between the Unitarian and Trinitarian principles, — which is, that according to the first, everything emanates from and is resolvable into *one essence*, and is included in *one sphere* ; while according to the second, all things emanate from and are resolvable into *two opposite essences*, to one of which *Heaven* is the sphere, or habitation, and to the other *Hell* ; — we do not mean to intimate that the theology of the Church is founded upon, or is supported by, *a Trinitarian Philosophy*. No such philosophy has ever been recognized by the Church, and we may say that none is now known to exist that is deserving of that name ; although many *philosophical works* may be found which *recognize the doctrine* of the Trinity. It is this that gives to the writer his *peculiar position* in offering this statement of a Universal Science or form of Universal Philosophy founded upon the Trinitarian principle.

As the Church is an institution calculated for the wants of man as he exists in an external natural condition, in which he cannot of course be capable of absolute cognition, and so cannot be made to *comprehend* spiritual truth ; the consequence is, that, while the truths that are committed to its charge by record and by tradition belong to a spiritual order, they are presented to mankind clothed in symbolic forms which are adapted to external natural comprehension, and addressed to the *sentimental nature* which can only *feel* or *apprehend,* and is dependent upon external natural thought and external natural experiences for a form or a statement through which these truths must be communicated to the natural mind.   By the necessity of its constitution, therefore, the Church is deprived of a rational basis in Philosophy, because the sentimental nature cannot recognize spiritual ideas except as they are translated into natural forms which are *opposite to them* while at the same time they *represent them.*

No consistency, therefore, can belong to the statements of the Church ; and no philosophy is possible for it except that which is hostile to it.   It is true that these statements have been supported by even an extraordinary display of *logical power,* because this external mode of argumentation belongs particularly to the external sphere of the soul's experience ; but although these statements have always been supported by an abundance of *reasoning,* this reasoning has been *deficient in Reason,* because based upon premises that are absurd.   This, however, is a necessity, and cannot possibly be avoided.   We therefore find that the Protestant Church, so long as it retains its original horror of Unitarianism, invariably manifests a decided hostility to Philosophy.   It is true that the Church of Rome is more tolerant of Philosophy than the Protestant Church,

7

for the reason that the element of good, or use, which is harmonious with Unitarianism, necessarily attracts a large share of its attention. But this Church is characterized above all others as *dogmatic*, and while it makes use of *all* philosophies so far as they can be made to support an argument in favor of her own dogmas, these philosophies have always been natural or Unitarian, and thus Pantheistic, because there has been no other. Thus Clemens Alexandrinus writes, " I do not call that Philosophy which either the Stoics, the Platonists, the Epicureans, or the Peripatetics, singly teach ; but whatever dogmas are found in each sect to be true, and conducive to the knowledge and practice of piety, and justice, *these collected into one system*, I call Philosophy." Indeed the Epicurean, which is a purely material philosophy, is the only Pagan system that did not meet with *decided patrons* among the fathers of the Church. The Platonic system, — as it recognized an antagonism between the rational principle and the passions and appetites, which favored the asceticism of the Church, and harmonized with its natural conceptions of antagonism between the flesh and the spirit ; and as it appeared to recognize a principle of *absolute evil*, and was so far harmonious with Christianity, — was at one time the most popular. Augustine contended that Plato was a Christian philosopher ; and a *union* of Platonic and Christian doctrines was attempted by Justin Martyr, Athenagoras, and Clemens Alexandrinus. Subsequently, the Stoic and Aristotelian became the favorite systems ; the latter of which was very generally adopted by the Scholastics who flourished from the eleventh to the sixteenth centuries. All this is matter of historical record, and shows, not only that the Church was compelled to make use of Pagan philosophies because no other could be had, but that it could not have had any rational foundation for its beliefs, because these philosophies were Pagan and thus antagonistic to Christianity.

A late Catholic writer while exposing the Pantheistic character of the Unitarian philosophies of the present day, has attempted to set up a distinction between these and the philosophy recognized by the Church that shall exonerate it from the same charge.* In answer to the question, " Is not God all things, the Universe itself ? " he says, " *Mediante* the creative act, yes, otherwise no ; because, conceived simply as real, necessary, and eternal Being, *ens reale et necessarium,* he is not conceived as productive, and no universe is or can be asserted. The difference between Philosophy and Pantheism lies precisely *in the creative act of God.* Pantheism asserts that real being is, and there stops, and in doing so asserts God as real and necessary Being and nothing else. Philosophy goes a step farther, and asserts, Real being is Creator, and in doing

* See Brownson's Review, January, 1850.

so asserts the Universe ; for existences are nothing but the creative act of God in its terminus, as is asserted in asserting creation out of nothing.   To say that God *non mediante* the creative act is the Universe, is not true, for then there is no universe ; to say that God *mediante* the creative act is all things, is the Universe, is true ; for then the Universe is not only asserted, but asserted in its true relation to God, as being only *from him, by him,* and *in him,* through the creative act bringing it, as our author would say, forth from potentiality into actuality.   There is no possible bridge from God as . real and necessary Being to *existence,* or from existence to him, but his creative act, and therefore we must either rest in Pantheism, or assert creation out of nothing."

It is evidently a distinction without a difference that is here relied upon, and nothing but a logical quibble. The development of God in the Universe, which is here asserted by our reviewer in saying that it is *"from him, by him, and in him,"* is the very essence of Pantheism ; for it supposes Spirit and Matter to be harmonious, or homogeneous, and to be the result of Infinite activity alone.   This convenient mode of realizing *a Finite Material* Universe from *an Infinite Spiritual* source alone, merely by pronouncing the word *causation,* has before been tried by M. Cousin, and as we shall have occasion presently to notice this fact, nothing more need now be said.

In applying the Law of Unity or Individuality to *Spirit* or *Life*, then, we realize God as an INFINITE PRINCIPLE, or as Infinite Wisdom and Infinite Love combined as one in Infinite Potency or Power. But as this, should we stop here, would confine him to a solitary existence, and preclude the possibility of any *creation* from him — because the Infinite does not include the Finite, but is, in every respect, *opposite* to it, as we have seen in reflecting upon the Unitarian Principle — we are forced to the conclusion that, in the forms or modes of his existence, *God is not simple but complex*, and that this Infinite Principle of Life is only *one element* in his Being. By the application of the Law of Unity, then, we realize the first Element, or the first Person, in God, and also realize the particular relation of this to the other elements of his existence as HOLY GHOST, or SPIRIT. To obtain a conception of the other elements contained in Him, and also to obtain a clearer conception of this by comparison with them, we must apply the Laws of Duality and Trinity, which, with that of Unity, constitute the Law of Tri-Personality taken as the foundation of our system.

DUALITY,

THE LAW OF PRODUCTION.

THE idea of Dualism was recognized by many of the ancient philosophers; although this was for the most part, and we may perhaps say always, merely a recognition and generalization of that *representative* dualism which is found to exist in Nature. Thus HERACLITUS maintained that "*every power in Nature and in Spirit must evolve an opposite as the sole means and condition of its manifestation,*" and that "*all opposition includes a tendency to reunion.*" But this was not a recognition of positive, or absolute, opposition; for it is not probable that Heraclitus admitted the supposition that Life must evolve its opposite Death, Truth its opposite Falsehood, or Good its opposite Evil; and if he had it would not make it the less absurd. It was only the recognition of a *natural fact*, that opposites always attract and unite together in manifestation, and the recognition of

the precedence of the male principle, or the evolution
of *Love* from *Wisdom* and their reunion in a three-fold
principle of *Individuality*; a fact which we see illustrated in the creation of the woman from the man, and in
the evolution of the body of the infant from the head
in the process of generation or development; a fact of
no particular importance, as the true relationship between these principles is settled by the statement of
the Law of Unity which establishes *Individuality* as a
three-fold form of *Body, Soul,* and *Spirit.*

According to Sharistan, an Arabian writer, "ZORO-
ASTER affirmed light and darkness, Yezdan and
Ahreman, to be two contrary principles, which were the
origin of everything subsisting in the world; the forms
of nature being produced by the combination of these
two principles; but maintained that the existence of
darkness is not to be referred to the one Supreme
Deity, who is without companion or equal, but must be
considered as the unavoidable consequence of his determination to create the world, in which light can no
more subsist without darkness, than a visible body can
exist without its shadow."

This, however, was a natural Unitarian, or Pantheistic, dualism that was more *poetical* than *philosophical*,
and only the incarnation of those opposite appearances
of good and evil which are incident to a natural
phenomenal existence; for, according to Zoroaster,
everything exists as an emanation from God. He says,

"Various orders of Spiritual Being, Gods, or Demons, have proceeded from the Deity which are more or less perfect as they are *at a greater or less distance in the course of emanation* from the eternal fountain of intelligence; among which the Human Soul is a particle of Divine Light which will *return to its source* and partake of its immortality; *and Matter is the last or most distant emanation from the first source of Being,* which, on account of its distance from the fountain of light, becomes opaque and inert, and while it remains in this state, *is the cause of evil;* but being gradually refined, it will at length return to the fountain whence it flowed."

The dualistic theory of PLATO was probably nothing more than the repetition in a new form of the old idea of Zoroaster. Both regarded the *Soul* of man as an emanation from God; or, rather as *a portion of Divine Substance;* and both regarded his *Body* as suggestive or productive of evil in consequence of its relation to *material substance.* Whether this material body derived its tendency to evil from its *remoteness* from the source of Light, or of Divine Life, from which it emanated, as taught by the former; or from "*an inherent refractory force,*" existing in material substance as an *opposite* to the Divine Life, as taught by the latter; is a matter of slight importance. Zoroaster regarded *the body* as destined to be re-united to, or absorbed into, its original fountain, as well as the soul; but Plato taught that *the soul only* was to be re-united to God, while *the*

8

body, together with the *passions* and *appetites*, which he
supposed to be connected with *the material portion of the
soul*, were temporary or destructible in their nature, and
were to be *got rid of* as soon as possible.

Neither of these philosophers taught, or probably
were able to realize the most distant conception of *the
resurrection of the body*; that is, *its regeneration as a
spiritual body*; because *this is a Christian idea*. They
only taught its *dissipation*, or *destruction*. The principle
of dualism as taught by Zoroaster was the most rational
of the two, because he did not, like Plato, fall into the
gross absurdity of regarding " *God and Matter as two
principles which are eternally opposite, not only differing in
their essences, but having no common principle by which
they can be united*," — and at the same time, suppose
CREATION *under such circumstances to be possible*, and
teach that *the body of man is* MATERIAL *and his Soul*
DIVINE. Even the facts of creation, and the co-opera-
tion of body and soul in manifestation, contradict such
a supposition, while Christianity of course rejects it because *founded in the idea of their union*.

An antagonistic dualism has also been recognized by
modern philosophers in the ideas of *Unity* and *Diversity*.
M. Cousin, the celebrated exponent of Eclecticism, and
one of the leading philosophers of the day, has attempted the reconciliation of these opposite ideas; but, having based his argument upon a natural phenomenal
ground, he has, of course, failed in this attempt. To

show how this dualism has been recognized by modern philosophers, and how M. Cousin has failed to accomplish the solution of this great metaphysical problem, I will quote from his " History of Philosophy." He says, " Human reason, whatever may be the mode of its development, however it begin, whatever it consider, whether it stop at the observation of that nature which lies around us, or plunge into the depths of the interior world, conceives all things only under the dominion of two ideas. Reason neither does nor can develope itself but under these two conditions. This division is but a reflection, under a more limited aspect, of that at which I rest ; and you may represent it to yourself under the formula of unity and multiplicity, of substance and phenomena, of absolute cause and relative causes, of the perfect and the imperfect, of the finite and the infinite. Each of these has two terms ; one of them necessary, absolute, *one*, substantial, causal, perfect, infinite ; the other, imperfect, phenomenal, relative, multiple, finite. A correct analysis identifies all these first terms together, and all these second terms together. It identifies immensity, eternity, absolute substance and absolute cause, perfection and unity, on the one hand ; and on the other, the multiple, the phenomenal, the relative, the limited, the finite, the bounded, the imperfect. We ought not to say, as is said by two great rival schools, that the human understanding begins either with Unity and the Infinite, or with the finite and the contingent, or multiple. In the order of the acquisition of our knowledge, the one supposes the other. You cannot separate variety from unity, nor unity from variety ; neither substance from phenomenon, nor phenomenon from substance ; one is anterior to the other, but does not exist without the other ; they co-exist necessarily. But how do they co-exist ? What is the mystery of this co-existence ? Unity is anterior to multiplicity, how, then, can unity admit multiplicity ? Human thought is unable to admit one without the other ; but in real order, we have seen that one is anterior to the other ; how, then, is this movement from unity to variety made ? Here is the fundamental vice of ancient and modern theories ; here is the vice of the theory of Kant. It places unity on one side, and multiplicity on the other ; and establishes such an opposition between them that all passage from one to the other seems impossible. A higher analysis resolves this contradiction.

We have identified all the first terms together and all the second terms together. And what are the first terms ? They are immensity, eternity, infinity, unity. We shall hereafter see how the school of Elis, placing itself at this point of view exclusively, at the summit of immensity, eternity, being in itself, and infinite sub-stance, defied all other schools to depart thence, and ever reach relative being, the finite, and multiplicity ; and mocked at those who admitted the existence of the world, which is only, after all, a great multiplicity.

The fundamental error of the school of Elis comes from this source, namely, that in all the first terms which we have enumerated, it forgot one which equals all the rest in certainty, and is entitled to the same authority as all the rest ; and that is the idea of *Cause*. Unity, or Substance, being an absolute cause, cannot but pass into act, cannot but develope itself. Take away the category of Causality from the other categories, the superficial observer discovers no omission of any importance ; but you may now perceive its consequences. It destroys every possible conception of the creation of the world. But unity, in itself, as absolute cause, contains the power of becoming variety and difference."

" What is the road that leads from God to the universe ? It is — creation. And what is creation ? What is it — to create ? — *not according to the hypothetical method, but the method we have followed — that method which always borrows from human consciousness that which, by a higher induction, it afterwards applies to the Divine Essence.* To create, is a thing which it is not difficult to conceive, for it is a thing which we do at every moment ; in fact, we create whenever we perform a free action. We create a free action ; we create it, I say, for we do not refer it to any principle superior to ourselves ; we impute it to ourselves exclusively. It was not ; it begins to be by virtue of that causality which we possess. Thus, to cause is to create ; but with what ? with nothing ? Certainly not. Man does not

draw forth from nothingness the act which he has not
yet done and is about to do ; he draws it forth from the
power which he has to do it, from himself.   Here is the
type of creation.   The divine creation is the same in its
nature.   God, if he is a cause, can create ; and if he is
an absolute cause, he cannot but create ; and in creating the universe he does not draw it forth from nothingness, but from Himself."

The reason why M. Cousin comes to a conclusion
opposite to the other philosophers here alluded to is,
that, while they contemplated the subject from an abstract philosophical ground, he contemplates it from a
practical empirical ground.   But, although he here
claims to have abandoned a hypothetical method that is
uncertain, for a practical method that is sure, because
he reasons from certain *facts of the consciousness ;* he has
evidently mistaken his own position both as to its nature and tendency.   He, as well as they, reasons hypo-
thetically because *he assumes that the consciousness of
freedom in the individual Will or personality of Man, is
equivalent to a conception of the law of causation, and draws
from this hypothetical premise his conclusion.*   The only
difference between them, then, is that they reason *legiti-
mately* while he reasons *absurdly.*   Reversing the order
of thought, he reasons from effect to cause, and not from
cause to effect, and thus is led to mistake a *natural
phenomenon* for a *spiritual law.*   This is a *double absurdity.*   It is absurd, in the first place, because we

can never understand a phenomenon until we have attained a perfect conception of the law which governs it. It is absurd, in the next place, because, as the natural is both *unconscious of*, and *opposite to*, the spiritual, a natural phenomenon cannot even become *suggestive* of a spiritual law, but must *contradict* it. If Pantheism were true, and God and Nature were perfectly harmonious, or homogeneous, this would not be quite so bad, although it would still be absurd; but as God and Nature are *opposite*, all conclusions drawn from such premises must be opposite to the truth. Even according to his own method, however, M. Cousin is inconsistent; for, while assuming the false position that man is a spiritual or absolute cause, and thus is *really a Creator*, and admitting the fact that he can create only from that which he finds in himself, he uses these as premises from which to draw the conclusion that God creates *the opposite of Himself*.

Another *peculiarity* of this writer is, that, being unable to rise above phenomenal appearances, he adopts the popular instead of the scientific definition of the principal terms upon which he undertakes to found his argument; rendering these terms entirely unfit for any philosophical use. Thus, instead of obtaining a conception of *the Finite Principle* — in which is included *the idea of Diversity*, and from which material substance and all natural imperfection are derived — he substitutes *the diversified forms of natural existence*, which

have been *redeemed from absolute diversity*, and thus
from finity, from chaos, or from death, by the operation
of an Infinite Unity.   Thus, instead of recognizing in
the ideas of Infinite and Finite, — Unity and Diversity,
— *two opposite absolute principles*, he sees in Diversity
only *the external of Unity*, and supposes the Finite to be
only *the development of the Infinite*, which would make
Nature, or *Creation*, to be, *not Natural, but Spiritual*.
Seeing that *Unity in diversity* is the *Law of natural life*,
and that imperfection is incidental to all the works of
creation, he has been led to infer that the Infinite and
Finite, that Unity and Diversity, *are in their essence, or
origin, one*.   M. Cousin has thus perpetrated the monstrous absurdity which we have declined to charge
against Heraclitus, and boldly asserted that an absolute
Infinite Cause must produce *from itself the opposite of
itself*.   The most unfortunate position assumed by this
writer, however, is that in which he professes to abandon " the hypothetical method," and attempts to obtain
a conception of *creation from an infinite spiritual cause*,
by referring to *the act of a finite natural phenomenon ;* —
to obtain a knowledge of *the modes of existence and
operation in God*, by referring to *the deceptive appearances
presented to the natural consciousness of man*.   This alone
would be sufficient to exclude M. Cousin from the
pale of Philosophy, and give to him the character of a
shallow empiric.

We should not have dwelt so long upon theories so

superficial were it not that this writer is one of the latest and most popular of modern philosophizers, and may by some be supposed to have succeeded in this attempt to harmonize, and to account for the conjunction of, those opposite principles which we find expressed by the terms Infinite and Finite, Unity and Diversity, to accomplish which has always been the great desideratum in Philosophy. Having seen that this fundamental dualism in existence has always been fully recognized, and that the secret of their union and combined manifestation in creation has never yet been discovered, but has always been regarded as the greatest of mysteries, we will proceed to the application of the *Law of Duality*, as here stated, in obtaining a conception of these opposite elements, and preparing the mind for their union and reconciliation and the realization of God as Father, Son, and Holy Ghost, by the application of the *Law of Trinity*.

According to our statement of the law of Duality, — As the condition of production, all things must exist in pairs as male and female, the first being characterized as *intellectual* and the second as *affectional ;* — and also in pairs as masculine and feminine, the first being characterized as *internal* and the second as *external ;* which dualities originally exist under a double and complex law of *affinity* and *antipathy*, and thus include the principles of *mutual attraction* and *mutual opposition.*

In applying this law of Duality for the purpose of
9

obtaining a conception of the nature of God without
any reference to previous thought, the first question
that would arise is this, — What are the most remote
principles or ideas of which we have any conception
that stand to each other in this compound relationship
of necessary attraction yet positive opposition ?   Now
we find that the most remote or abstract ideas which
we have of the *essences* or *causes* of things have always
been expressed by the terms SPIRIT and MATTER ;
and by matter we do not of course mean matter as it
appears in the diversified forms of creation, but the
material susceptibility, originally chaotic, that is recognized in philosophy.   These ideas of Spirit and Matter,
however, which have always been resorted to as a foundation for philosophy and theology, will be much better
expressed by the terms INFINITE and FINITE, because, although spirit and matter are *referable to* Infinite
and Finite principles they do not comprehend these
principles but are comprehended by them.   As it is
precisely to these that we are also directed by the
recognition of the Infinite Life, or Spirit, as the first
person in God, — because Finite is universally recognized as the opposite of Infinite, — we cannot but
accept these terms and recognize these principles as
the most remote causes from the union of which a conception of the second person in God is to be realized.
We have only to determine the question, What are the
attributes which belong to them ?   Very little definite

thought has ever been connected with these ideas, so vast are they in their nature, so opposite are they to all our *natural* conceptions, and so faintly do they present themselves to the consciousness. Although the terms Infinite and Finite have always been recognized by the best authorities as *opposite,* still, in defining the term Finite, nothing but a popular definition has been given that is applicable only to *the phenomena of natural exist- ence,* and is the same that is given to the term *definite.* Both these terms are used to express that which is *visible,* or is *defined to us by being made perceptible,* and both are defined to be " *that which is limited, or bounded."* Now it is correct to use the term finite in its *popular sense* as applied to natural phenomena, or to that which is limited or bounded, for the reason that the natural is supported by, and representative of, the finite principle, and is thus opposite or opposed to God. But "that which is limited or bounded" is no definition of the term finite. It is not so, because the finite, abstractly considered, is neither limited nor bounded, — because, being absolutely, or really, opposite to the Infinite, it is a *spiritual idea,* and so cannot be described by, or in- cluded in, a *natural term,* — and because this definition does not include any internal attribute or active charac- teristic that can affect *the character* of anything to which it is applied ; so that it is a sort of negative description that is philosophically useless. In defining these terms we would, therefore, say, that the elements of the INFINITE, according to the most general analysis, are, *Unity, Universality, Life ;* and that the elements of the FINITE are *Diversity, Partiality, Death, — the definite manifestations* of the first being *Truth, Good, Beauty,* while those of the second are *Falsehood, Evil, Deformity.* That this is the rational or scientific sense of these terms we think will be demonstrated by the result of their application to philosophic use. In stating our hypothesis, however, we have of course a right to assume them to be so.

All these conclusions are the necessary result of the first step taken by us. Having realized the conception of God as INFINITE SUBSTANCE, if we recognize in this substance the attributes of Universality and Individuality, or Unity, as applied to Truth, to Love, and to Life, — and no one can help doing this, — the conclusion must inevitably follow, in view of the fact of creation, that, *as the condition* of this creation, a substance *in everything opposite* to Infinite must have existed and have possessed the capacity of becoming receptive and productive from this opposite Infinite Principle ; for it must be palpably evident to all who understand the meaning of the terms used to express these attributes of Infinite Existence, that if this had not been so, *nothing but* Infinite Substance could ever have existed ; because as *unity, universality,* and *life,* are essential to the idea of Infinite, *diversity, partiality, imperfection, hate,* and *destruction,* or *death,* are necessarily *excluded,* and a natural creation, to which *these are essential,* and indeed production or creation of any kind, becomes impossible. There cannot be a more self-evident fact than this, that an *Infinite Principle* cannot alone, or of itself, create, or be productive. According to the universally accepted meaning of this term, the idea of production from it involves a palpable contradiction, absurdity, or impossibility. It is impossible, I repeat, because, according to this acceptation, the Infinite Principle, as LIFE ITSELF, including the essence and cause of all *Truth,* of all *Good,* and of all *Beauty,* existing in the union of WISDOM ITSELF with LOVE ITSELF, is understood to include *unity* and *universality* as elementary characteristics, and is thus *opposite* to the ideas of *diversity,* of *partiality,* of *divisibility,* and *visibility,* which we know are requisites in production. This being granted, it must be seen, because it plainly follows as a necessary consequence, that a principle *in everything the opposite* of Infinite, and therefore existing as DEATH ITSELF, including the essence and cause of all *Falsehood,* of all *Evil,* and of all *Deformity or Imperfection,* must have existed as furnishing THE ONLY POSSIBLE MATERIAL FOR CREATION. We have perhaps dwelt longer upon this idea than is necessary; but the writer wishes to invite particular attention to this statement, because the central principles upon which his whole system is founded will be seen to grow out of it; and if its

necessity, however repulsive it may seem, should not
be recognized, it would be useless to proceed any further in attempting to *comprehend* either the nature of
Being, the spiritual ideas of Christianity, or the nature,
relationships, and destination of the Human Soul.

In applying the Law of Duality to absolute existence, or absolute substance, then, we have demonstrated
the necessity that two opposite spiritual or absolute
principles, substances, or causes, must have existed as
the condition of Creation. But although Dualism is
the Law of Production, as this dualism supposes *opposition* and not union, before any production could
possibly take place two things become necessary.
First, as these opposite Infinite and Finite substances
belong to, or rather *constitute*, opposite spheres, one of
Life, and the other of *Death*, so that *neither could be conscious of the other*, the necessity arises that these should
become *combined in one consciousness, or in one individual ;*
because if it were otherwise, there could be no conscious communication between them, and so no use
made of that material substance which is an element
in the Finite, and must furnish the material for, and
constitute the body of, Existence. It next becomes
necessary that, as *the first condition* of creation, a
DIVINE SUBSTANCE should be formed from *the
union* of these opposite spiritual substances in this
individual, so that he should, by combining in himself
the opposite poles of existence, Life and Death, —

Infinite and Finite, — Unity and Diversity, — Good and Evil, — as Soul and Body, or Substance and Form, so that the lower should be subjected to the higher principle for use, — *realize the consciousness of all possible things*, and thus constitute the Soul of the Universe as well as the Soul of Deity. THE FATHER by whom all things are to be created would thus become separated from the Infinite Life or Spirit as a *Living Principle* constituting *the second Person* in the Godhead.

This union of absolute opposite principles is made *possible* in the fact of *attraction* recognized in our statement of the Law of Duality, an attraction that arises in the adaptation there is in Finite Substance to furnish to the Infinite, *material* for creation, and thus for a mutual realization, or expression. It also is made *practicable* by the combination of these opposite principles in one individual in whom the *finite Love*, — if such a term can be used to express the animating power of finite existence, which *resists* creation because it is the essence of death or destruction, — *could be sacrificed*. The *necessity* of this union as the condition of creation has already been demonstrated. It is a remarkable phenomenon that a fact so palpably necessary and self-evident should have so long been overlooked, especially as it has been *represented* in all created existences, and has been *proclaimed* in the most unequivocal manner in the Scriptures. It must be accounted for upon the ground that the knowledge of this fact has not before been *necessary,* and so its recognition has not been permitted. If we take the following declarations found in Paul's Epistle to the Romans and in the Book of Ecclesiasticus in connection, we have a complete *promulgation* of the Law of Duality as it has here been stated, and a decided *recognition* of the union of opposite absolute principles in God here seen to be necessary.

" For the invisible things of him from the foundation of the world are clearly seen, being understood by the things that are made, even his Eternal Power and Godhead." " Good is set against Evil, and Life against Death. So is the godly against the sinner and the sinner against the godly. So look upon all the works of the most High, and there are two and two, one against the other."

This, it will be seen, is a distinct recognition of a universal representative Dualism, including a double antagonism of principles corresponding precisely with the Law of Duality as here stated, and referring to an absolute dualism in God. Indeed words cannot well express a confirmation more complete. So far, however, we have only shown *the necessity* for the union of these opposite absolute principles. By the application of this Law of Duality we have only realized *their combination in one individual,* so that their union and the realization of a Divine Substance, has become *a possibility.* It must be evident, that, in consequence of this meeting of opposite spiritual principles or forces in one individual, there must have resulted an absolute opposition in him as of death to life, — a dualism partaking of the characteristics of, and representing in definite forms, the Infinite and Finite principles from which they were derived. This individual must, therefore, have realized in himself an opposition of principles, both intellectually and affectionally, which, *while it constituted his freedom*, must, so long as this opposition continued, *have prevented any marriage in him*, and thus have prevented the realization, or formation of that Divine Substance upon which creation depended, so that no production from him would have been possible. It will therefore be seen that we have gone as far as the Law of Duality will carry us in realizing a conception of the nature of God, and that we are thus led to the consideration of the third division of our subject, which is the application of the Law of Trinity.

10

TRINITY,

THE LAW OF LIFE.

THE idea of Trinity has never been stated as a philosophic formula, or applied as a law of Life. It is only found in the Scriptures, — where it is taught, or at least suggested, as a form of existence in God, — and in the Church, which was instituted as the interpreter of these Divine records according to natural forms of thought and modes of conception to those who are confined to an external natural sphere of consciousness. Here, therefore, it appears as a theological dogma only, which is totally unfit for any philosophic use. A three-fold personality in God, as Father, Son, and Holy Ghost, is here *assumed* as a theological fact; but the particular relationship subsisting between these persons has never, in the Church, been considered as a subject for thought, but only the relationship that exists between these several persons and the Human Soul, which was created after their image. Thus the Father has been invested with the character of *Creator, Preserver,* and *Governor ;* — the Son, with the character of *Redeemer,* — and the Holy Ghost with the character of *Sanctifier.* It has been assumed that the first man, having committed an *infinite offence* by disobeying the command of his Creator, had become liable, — and with him the whole human race descending from him, — to the infliction of an *infinite punishment ;* this being a state of everlasting misery and woe expressed as an eternity of torment in Hell. That, in this state of affairs, the Son, being excited by compassion for the miserable condition and prospects of Humanity, was induced to *assume* this load of guilt with which Humanity was burthened, and to pay the penalty which was demanded of them by the Father ; and that this he did by becoming incarnated in a human form, and voluntarily yielding up his life upon the Cross. It has further been assumed, that, in consequence of this sacrifice by the Son, the human race has been relieved from all imputation of the original sin of the first man, so that it has become *possible* for us to receive the sanctifying influence of the Holy Ghost, — to become reconciled to God through the merits of Christ, — and to become inheritors of eternal happiness with Him. That, being free, man has still the power to receive or to reject this holy influence which is continually soliciting for admission into his heart. That, if within the period of his natural life, which is by them *limited to this atmosphere,* he consents to receive it, he is saved ; but should he *" die and make no sign,"* he is deprived of the benefit of Christ's sacrifice, and suffers the penalty originally denounced against the disobedient. *What constitutes* the sign of grace and deliverance, is, of course, the great topic of dispute ; but this is always some particular form of belief, or of practice, which is varied in each particular denomination or portion of the Church.

Although all the doctrines of each one of these particular denominations of Christianity are founded in this conception of the Tri-Personality of God, — or, rather, upon this conception of *the modes* in which these persons *manifest* themselves in relation to the human race, — which gives to them their designation of Trinitarian ; this conception does not come within the sphere of Rationality, or even of Morality, — is limited entirely to the sphere of Religion as a theological dogma, — and, being a natural form of thought in which *diversity* is a necessary element, degenerates into the worship of three distinct persons, and so into the worship of three gods, which never can be conceived as constituting one.

Such being the imperfection of these statements of Trinity as a theological dogma, it is not surprising that, as the religious sentiment upon which it is dependent for its support loses its predominance by the increased demand for rationality, and for a morality that is more congenial with self-conscious right and sympathetic feeling, than with a blind obedience to law, — there should be found a prevailing disposition to evade such absurdities by the introduction of some substitute.

The idea of Tri-Unity, which has already been described in treating of Unity as the Law of Individuality, has sometimes been set up as a substitute for that of Trinity by the enemies of that which is representative of spiritualism in the Church ; not with the idea of founding upon it any theological system, for which it is entirely unfit, but for the purpose ¡ of accounting, or *seeming* to account, for a doctrine so extensively recognized in the Church ; and always, probably, with the intention of subverting the original doctrine, and with it the peculiar dogmas which have been founded upon it.

This idea of Tri-Unity, however, is not even *the representative* of any spiritual idea, but is only the partial recognition of *a natural phenomenon*, or of a natural law which may be found manifested in an infinite variety of forms. Although generally stated as Wisdom, Love, and Power, corresponding with the three most general divisions of the *consciousness*, which includes an Intellectual, an Affectional, and an Active principle ; it has also been stated, — probably for the sake of novelty, — as " the *knower*, the *known*, and the *act of knowing* ; " — corresponding with the three most general divisions of the *Intellect*, which are Intuition, Sensation, and Reflection ; and with the three general divisions of the *Understanding*, which is made up of Perceptive, Receptive, and Reflective faculties ; — three elements which are found to co-exist in every thought, and even in the most simple perception of the intellect.

Although these statements, corresponding with the Law of Unity, or Individuality, are more in harmony with rationality than the discordant statement of Trinityism which it would supersede ; it is a rationality belonging to a natural sphere of thought ; and instead of being, like that, the recognition of modes of existence and manifestation in God, are only the recognition of modes of existence and manifestation in *the human mind ;* or rather of the most general aspect, or superficial individualization, of its forms and operations, which have no reference to, and cannot become suggestive of, any spiritual idea. Both in a theological and in a spiritual sense, therefore, they are not only entirely worthless, but are antagonistic or destructive.

Individuals in endeavoring to trace the origin of the idea of Tri-Personality in the Church, — being impressed with the notion that there is not a sufficiency of evidence in the Scriptures to warrant such an idea, and overlooking or denying the fact that the Church has other grounds besides the Scriptures upon which this and other truths of Christianity rest, — such as the unrecorded traditions of the Church, and the sentimental intuitions and recognitions of its members, — are very apt to suppose, or at least find it *very convenient to assert*, that it is upon some of these natural forms of a three-fold individuality, that the Church has founded its doctrine of Tri-Personality. Some, indeed, have gone so far as to insinuate that this doctrine is only a modification, or *corruption*, of an idea found in the Pagan mythologies of India and of Scandinavia.

If we look attentively, however, at any of these natural substitutes, it will be seen that, while they represent *the form* of this idea, they are *opposed to its substance* ; and that in all the philosophies and mythologies of Pagan nations, however much the form of Deity may be multiplied, their *Unitarianism* will appear in the idea of *emanation* from, and resolvability into, *some one central principle* ; and their natural character will appear in the difference, or discordance, which attends the attributes and the manifestations of these Deities.

Thus we read in the Laws of Menu, which form a part of the Hindoo Scriptures, " Let every Brahmin with fixed attention consider all nature, both visible and invisible, as existing in the Divine Spirit ; for, when he contemplates the boundless universe existing in the Divine Spirit, he cannot give his heart to iniquity."

" The Divine Spirit is the whole assemblage of Gods ;

all worlds are seated in the Divine Spirit; and the Divine Spirit, no doubt, produces the connected series of acts performed by embodied souls."

" But he must consider the Supreme Omnipresent Intelligence as the Sovereign Lord of them all; a Spirit which can only be conceived by a mind slumbering; but which he may imagine more subtil than the finest conceivable essence, and more bright than the purest gold. Him some adore as transcendently present in elementary fire; others in Menu, lord of creatures; some as more distinctly present in Indra, regent of the clouds and the atmosphere; others in pure air; others as the Most High Eternal Spirit."

The idea of two natures, or principles, including a positive opposition the same in character as that between Heaven and Hell, being made to exist as one through Sacrifice, is an idea peculiar to Christianity, and cannot be found anywhere else; except, as we have said, that all things of the Spirit must be unconsciously repre-sented in the phenomena of natural life which are in substance opposite to Spirit, but which from this simi-larity of form are liable to be mistaken for it. We might as well expect to discover life by poring into death, or to discover the *laws* of nature simply by gen-eralizing the *phenomena* of nature, as expect to discover in any Pagan or Unitarian statement a single form of absolute truth, or indeed to find anything except a perfect *contradiction* to this truth. These interrogations

11

of nature are similar to those interrogations of the ora-
cles of old, whose responses were sought with *the understanding* that they would be *deceptive,* keeping the word
of promise to the ear to break it to the hope. Nature is
always so deceptive. It is only by obtaining a position
above her that we can ever hope to *understand* her, or
find in her anything more than a phantasmagoria of
shadows which are deceptive, unsubstantial, and vain.

The dogma of the Church, then, upon which such
monstrous superstitions as those here described have
been built, and which we are required by her to believe
without the possibility of ever understanding, would
seem to be the only legitimate representative that has
ever been offered of the fact of Tri-Personality in God ;
for, until Christianity has been *expressed* in the form of
an exact philosophy, instead of being *represented* in the
many-colored garment of a discordant theology, *no substitute* can be found for this dogma that will not prove
to be destructive to the *Idea* that it is made to represent.

Having considered the various substitutes which
have been offered for the idea of Tri-Personality in
God, we will proceed to the application of the Law of
Trinity, as it has here been stated, for the purpose of
realizing this idea not only as a *theological dogma,* but
also as a *philosophical fact,* from the application of which
a system of theology will result that shall be perfectly
harmonious in itself, while at the same time it will em-

brace all the particular denominations of Christianity which have heretofore been so discordant.

By the application of the Law of Unity, we have succeeded in realizing Infinite Life as the first Personality in God ; this being characterized as SPIRIT, and corresponding with the HOLY GHOST, as recognized by the Church.

By the application of the Law of Duality, we have succeeded in realizing, as the only condition under which creation could be possible, *the combination in one Individual* of this Infinite Life with an opposite Finite Principle ; and thus have realized *the possibility* of a Divine Substance that shall constitute the Soul of Deity as FATHER, or CREATOR, as well as the Soul of the Universe.

In doing this, however, we have realized in this Individual an antagonistic dualism which must have prevented marriage in him, and so have prevented any production from him ; which renders imperative the application of some other law that shall produce a harmonious manifestation of Intellect, of Affection, and of Will, and also make him *at-one* with the Infinite Life, so that he may constitute A LIVING PRINCIPLE capable of communicating this life to the material organizations of created existence. This we shall find is provided in the Law of Trinity. According to our statement of this law, — As the condition of Absolute Life, and thus of permanency, or perpetuity, all things must become one

with absolute unity by the union of opposites produced
by the *sacrifice of individualism*, or selfism, and recognizing Infinite Wisdom and Infinite Love as the life of
all things, become a *three-fold personality* existing in
three several spheres of consciousness made one as
Body, Soul, and Spirit.

The principle of Individualism, or Selfism, the sacrifice of which is demanded by the Law of Trinity, is
the principle of SELF-LOVE. It is the affective principle, or motive power, that belongs to the Finite Principle, and so must accompany all that is born out of the
Finite, as well as everything whose existence partakes
of a finite character ; — and being *opposite* to the Universal Love of the Infinite Life, is a *destructive* or *anti-
productive* principle or force. This sacrifice is demanded because a state of *absolute dualism*, or the consciousness of both infinite and finite existence, which
must always precede the realization either of absolute
life, or of absolute death, or damnation, necessarily
includes the conscious presence of *two opposite Loves*.
Now as one of these loves has an affinity for life, and
production, and the other for death, and destruction ;
and as two such loves cannot remain together, or be
entertained together by any individual, any more than
he can entertain both love and hate for the same thing
at the same time, *one of these loves must be sacrificed.*
In this case, then, in order that a Divine Substance
should have been realized as Father, or Creator, *a free*

choice must have been made by this Individual of an Infinite Love as his only animating and productive power ; the consequence of which would be, that the Self-Love that would reject the Infinite Wisdom, would destroy or expel the Infinite Love, and resist the Infinite Production, — would be sacrificed or expelled by Infinite Force.

I would here pause, and urge upon the reader the great importance of obtaining a clear comprehension of the necessity for the meeting and conflict of these two opposite Loves *before any individual can realize a state of absolute freedom,* or be placed in a position which makes it *possible* that he should become one either with a Divine, or with an Infernal Principle : Also that he should see the necessity that, under such circumstances, either Self-Love or the Love of God should *immediately* be sacrificed in him ; because this recognition is essential not only to the existence of the system here to be presented, but also to the existence of all that is vital in Christianity. It will hereafter be shown, not only that the fact that we are able to love many things which are vastly dissimilar, and even *opposite* in a natural sense, is no obstacle to the reception of this idea ; but that even the fact that the Love of God and Self-Love may *both* be made to operate *at the same time* through *the same individual* does not affect it ; there being necessarily contained in the unregenerated soul after the fact of election has taken place, and its redemption accomplished, as these terms will hereafter be explained, spheres of reception and mediums of manifestation which are not only dissimilar, but *spiritually opposite ;* for if this were not so, regeneration would be unnecessary. This is because the soul, having become one with the spiritual, or with absolute life, exists in three several spheres of consciousness, and these cannot be made perfectly one as Body, Soul, and Spirit, until *an entire regeneration* of its natural organization shall have been effected; and thus, although Self-Love may have been sacrificed *at the centre* of the will, it may still be found to operate *at the circumference.* This fact is taught most explicitly by St. Paul, and is made possible because the Will, even in its most concentrated form, is not a simple power acting through a single organ, but is a *complex power* of the soul; or rather, *is* the soul manifesting itself in a *complex manner* through a trinity of organs which belong to different regions of the mind and spheres of thought and affection, constituting man a three-fold personality corresponding with the three-fold personality of God.

In returning to our subject we find that by the union in one Individual of Infinite and Finite Substance, which constitute the opposite poles of existence, and the sacrifice in the individual, *where it first comes in con-scious contact with its opposite,* of that finite or partial love which is the essence, fountain, and source of self-love — selfishness — or self-ism, — we have realized

a Divine Substance as FATHER or CREATOR, in whom two
opposite natures have been made one, and a unity of
Life, of Love, and thus of Will, realized, by which that
which constitutes Body has become subject to the Soul
for use ; and in whom, therefore, *all the possibilities of
creation* must have been realized as a DIVINE IDEA.

We are, therefore, in some measure made to compre-
prehend the position and relationship of this Divine
Person as the Soul of Deity, and the substance or sus-
taining power of the Created Universe. We cannot,
however, stop here, because our statement of the Law
of Trinity demands a realization of consciousness in
THREE spheres made one, as Body, Soul, and Spirit,
while we have as yet realized only the Spirit and the
Soul. *An external principle proceeding from the Father,*
and thus designated as *the Son,* is therefore now demanded.

The evolution of the body from the head, which is
relatively soul, in the process of generation, to which I
have already alluded, and the order of development in
the human soul, as this will hereafter be described, are
natural representatives of this great spiritual fact ; but
had not this fact been first realized in God, as the operation of a Law of Being, it could never have been represented in nature. As the production from an internal
sphere of absolute existence of an external sphere corresponding to it as body to soul, and the union of these
through sacrifice with the Infinite Life, are demanded

by the Universal Laws which have here been stated,
and which *nothing can be found to contradict* ; although
THE IDEA of creation was a necessary realization in the
Father as Divine Substance, THE FACT of creation would
not have been possible without a complete Trinity of
Persons in the Godhead.   These laws demand an external principle, as *Body,* in the SON, and an internal
principle, as *Soul,* in the FATHER, united *as One*
through sacrifice with the Infinite Principle of Life,
which is the HOLY GHOST.

Up to this point we have not been obliged to depend
for any support upon the statement of Universal Laws
taken as the foundation of our system ; because we have
been sustained by internal *self-evident* truths which are
abundantly sufficient.   Even now, we do not need this
support, because the existence of the Son as a person
distinct from the Father has always been recognized
both by Unitarians and Trinitarians as a fact distinctly
taught in the Scriptures.   It is true that the former
refuse to acknowledge in the Son the existence of those
attributes which belong to him as a person in the
Trinity ; but language must constitute a very poor
medium for the expression of thought, if the quotations
here introduced from the Scriptures to illustrate the
character of the Son do not, according to their own
mode of interpretation, declare this character and relationship to be precisely what it has here been represented, and that in the most explicit and unmistakable

manner. The mind must be severely ruled by the Fancy at the expense of the Reason, which, while recognizing the Scriptures as a true record or revelation, refuses to acknowledge the Divinity of the Son, or his reality as a mode of existence in God. Those, however, who have gone along with us so far, and have perceived the soundness of our conclusions, will probably find no difficulty in continuing to the end, or at least in admitting the necessity for this third person in God.

The spiritual and natural elements which constituted this most external personality in God, or most external sphere of existence, as internal and external, must, of course, have been made one with Infinite Life, and thus have become living and productive as a *spiritual* Tri-Unity, by the same kind of sacrifice which produced the *Divine* Tri-Unity first realized. It was this that constituted him, as the Scriptures have declared, *" the Lamb slain before the foundation of the world ; "* for this declaration is not *prospective,* having reference to his subsequent incarnation and crucifixion ; but is a literal statement having reference to the formation of that Tri-Personality which alone made " the foundation of the world " *possible.* This is also taught in the following words, " For it pleased the Father that in him all fullness should dwell ; and *having made peace by the blood of the Cross,* by him to reconcile all things unto himself : by him I say, whether they be *things in Earth,* or *things in Heaven."* For, although the *" things in earth "* relate

12

to the subsequent formation of a Divine-Human or Spiritual sphere by the *incarnation* of the Son, which will next be explained, and which was consummated by a sacrifice of which his visible crucifixion was only a type, — the *" things in Heaven,"* which were also reconciled to God by the blood of the Cross, evidently relate to the formation of that heavenly sphere which followed the consummation of a Tri-Personality in God. This explains the meaning of these words which came to Jesus when he prayed to the Father that he would glorify his Name, or glorify his Son. " Then came there a voice from Heaven, saying, I have both glorified it, and will glorify it again." This is evidently the recognition of a *past* glorification consequent upon the reconciliation to the Father of the *" things in Heaven "* by the sacrifice of *" the Lamb of God,"* and also the recognition of a *promised* glorification consequent upon the reconciliation to him of the *" things in earth "* by the sacrifice of *" the Son of Man."* Thus Jesus afterwards said, " And now Father glorify thou me with thine own self; with the glory which I had with thee before the world was."

This demand for a Tri-Personality in God by the Law of Trinity as it has here been stated and applied, may thus be seen to be legitimate, not only because everything in natural existence will be found to *represent* it, but because it is supported by the most explicit declarations of the Scriptures. In describing the creation of the world, God is here represented as saying, " Let *us* make man in *our Image,* after *our Likeness*." Now this evidently *supposes,* not only that the Father, or Creator, is here addressing a person *distinct from himself,* and is not speaking *to himself,* but also supposes that the Father, *as we have here represented him,* — a Divine Substance, containing in himself *all the possibilities* of Creation, or the Creation as a *Divine Idea,* — is addressing *the Son* as we have here represented him, and as the Scriptures repeatedly represent him, — that is, as the *external embodiment* or definite expression of that which exists in the Father; precisely as a *Thought* is the embodiment of an *Idea.* It will certainly so appear if we take in connection the following words of St. Paul : —

" God, who at sundry times, and in divers manners, spake in time past unto the fathers by the prophets, hath in these last days spoken to us by *his Son* whom he hath appointed heir of all things, by whom also *he made the worlds ;* who, being the brightness of his glory, and the express image of his person, when he had by himself purged our sins, sat down on the right hand of the Majesty on high ; being made so much better than the angels, as he hath by inheritance obtained a more excellent name than they. For unto which of the angels said he at any time, Thou art my Son, this day have I begotten thee ? Of the angels he saith, who maketh his angels spirits, and his ministers a flame of fire. But unto the Son he saith, Thy throne, O God, is for ever and ever : a sceptre of righteousness is the sceptre of thy kingdom."

Although the statement of Tri-Personality in God that has here been made, may not now convey to the reader this idea as it exists in the mind of the writer ; should he follow in the path into which this statement will lead, and see how all the ideas which are but rudely and discordantly *represented* by the theology of the Churches are evolved from it, or produced as *necessary consequences,* and thus made perfectly harmonious ; its importance in an *abstract* point of view will be seen. And should he follow still further, — should he descend with us into the region of Psychology, and witness the *illustrations* of this idea presented by the various conditions and operations of the human mind which this statement has enabled us to realize, — it will become still clearer to his mind, and the importance in a *practical* point of view of the statement here made of it, will be still more apparent ;   for, as all things are created as images, or representatives, of this three-fold Personality in God, — or of his modes of existence and manifestation under this form, — it not only furnishes a key that enables us to comprehend the great truths of Christianity, but a principle of classification and analysis also, that will be useful in the investigation of all departments of knowledge, both scientific and philosophical ; while in the investigation of the nature of the *human mind,* it is indispensable to success.

The origin and the nature of Evil, both positive and negative, — that is, both that which is absolute, or real, as well as that which is relative, or phenomenal, — will be accounted for and made comprehensible, and all the conflicting opinions which have prevailed upon this subject be completely reconciled.

There cannot be a more perplexing subject, or one upon which less satisfactory or more discordant conclusions have been entertained, than that of *the Origin of Evil ;* and this perplexity is increased by the fact, that all the various and opposite theories which have been constructed upon this subject are in *some sense* true, while in another sense they are *opposite* to the truth, so that the truth can really be obtained only by the means of a statement that will not only *account for,* but *include* and *reconcile* them all.

For instance, it is both true and false that Evil originates in God, — both true and false that it originates in Man, — both true and false that it originates in and proceeds only from the Devil. It is both true and false that Evil is nothing but the result of *natural imperfection* and thus only nominal and not real, — only phenomenal and not absolute, being always calculated for and ending in the production of good, — as the Pantheists assert. It is also both true and false that Evil is a sin against an Infinite Being which must be visited by an infinite, eternal, punishment, and result in a constantly increasing degradation that is further and further *removed* from Good, — as the Church teaches.

Although these notions are all, in their turn, useful as *sentimental experiences* with which the understanding has nothing to do ; no approach towards the truth can be obtained by the demonstration of any one of them, or use gained by its application ; because a partial or one sided truth when applied universally, or in any degree out of its own sphere, will not direct, but mislead us ; and will, therefore, always be productive of false theories. It is only when we understand *in what sense* it is that these notions are *all true,* and in what sense they are *all false,* that we can really *know* anything about them, or be safe in adopting them as general principles either for theoretical or practical use. The reconciliation of these opposite opinions is one of the incidental effects which will be found to result from the application of this statement of the Trinitarian Principle.

Although the idea of Evil existing, or ever having existed, in the nature of God, is at the first view a repulsive one, it will here be shown to be *inseparable* from any true idea of God, of Spiritualism, or of Christianity. It is not, however, an idea peculiar to this system, but one that is in harmony with statements made by the founders of Protestantism, to whom we must look for spirituality *in Idea,* however natural and crude may have been their *statements* of it. It is also in harmony with the declarations of the Scriptures. We here find God, as the Father, or Creator, asserting himself thus. "I am Jehovah, and none else ; beside me there is no God : Forming *Light* and creating *Darkness*, — making *Peace* and *creating Evil :* I, Jehovah, am the *Author* of all these things."

It is not, of course, possible that God should have been the author of Evil, or even have obtained any knowledge of its existence, had it not at some time been a fact of his own *consciousness,* or formed a part of his own *experience.* The fact that consciousness, or knowledge, is inseparable from *identity,* so that individuals *can become cognizant of phenomena only so far as the principles or laws which govern these phenomena are present in them, or are referable to some element of their nature,* is covered by or included in that part of our statement of Duality as the Law of Production which demands the union of an external with an internal principle ; and will be most amply illustrated and demonstrated in the course of this work, as nothing can be produced or manifest itself except upon this condition. If this has not yet been received as an axiom in philosophy, it has been recognized as a fact of the consciousness. Those individuals, therefore, who have endeavored to be consistent in carrying out the Unitarian Idea into its more remote consequences, and to whom God is, of course, a simple and not a complex Being, — have been compelled to accept the conclusion

that, as it is not possible that God should ever have
been conscious of Evil *in himself,* it is not possible
that he should ever be conscious of its existence *in
others,* and, therefore, that he can have no knowledge
of the punishment which *of itself* it inflicts upon the
offender.

In the statement that has here been made, I have
endeavored to demonstrate *the necessity* that God should
exist as a Tri-Personality; and I do not hesitate to
affirm not only that this Tri-Personality must result
from the application of the triple law of Being stated
as the foundation of our system, but that it is a
self-evident proposition which must arise in the simple
recognition of the existence of God as an Infinite principle of Life.   That the Tri-Personality here realized is
a *legitimate* one that is distinguished from, and opposed
to, the Unitarian idea of *Tri-Unity,* — Trinity of *Elements,* — or Trinity of *Operations,* — I think must be
conceded.   The fact that the Finite principle must
always exist in its original integrity, — that it may
operate as the animating principle, or furnish the
motive power, to all natural life, which cannot exist
without being supported by Self-ism, or Self-Love,
originating partiality, hate, destructiveness, etc., which
cannot flow into it, or come to it, from God ; — and also
that it may furnish the source from which an Infernal
sphere that we call Hell, can be sustained, precisely as
the sphere of Heaven is sustained by the *Infinite* activ-

ity, — precludes the idea of a simple individuality in God ; for it shows that the creating power of the universe *could not be a combination* of Infinite and Finite force simply, but must have been produced *out of the Finite* by the Infinite, and exist as a separate power, person, or individuality. This would necessitate a *Duality*, while the application of the Law which demands an external as well as an internal principle as the condition of production, — which, besides being a self-evident proposition, can be proved to exist as a Universal Law, creation being formed as an image of this mode of existence in God, — necessitates that *Tri-Personality* which the Church has always with great consistency and pertinacity contended for as essential to her existence ; and rightly so because all the doctrines which distinguish Christianity from Paganism have been constructed by her from a statement of this idea.

As, according to the statement here made, the three persons who constitute God bear the relation to each other of *Body*, *Soul*, and *Spirit*, a perfect Unity, or substantial Individuality is the result ; and the character and relationship of these persons, as well as the intercourse between them, are rendered perfectly comprehensible by the human mind. They are made comprehensible, — first, because they correspond with universal laws, of which we may observe in nature a great variety of illustrations ; — again as they corres-

13

pond with the three several spheres of *individuality* as
manifested through the Will, where the higher elements
descend and become more definitely expressed or
manifested in the lower; — and lastly as they are
represented by the three several spheres of *consciousness,* or kinds of life, designated as external, internal,
and spiritual, into which the soul successively enters.
Each one of these possesses an individuality and a
consciousness peculiarly its own, — perfectly distinct
although perfectly analogous, — and calculated to act
as one.   They are thus perfectly representative of those
three descending spheres of life which have here been
represented as constituting the Tri-Personality in which
God exists.   The soul is so constituted not only because
God said " Let us make man in our image," but because
were it not so there could be no bond of union, or medium of communication, between man and the Infinite
source of Life ; and thus no resurrection for him to a
Spiritual Life which is one with it.

As there seems to be an objection in some minds to
the use of the word *persons* as applied to God, it may
be well here to state that *form* is not necessarily
included in, or connected with, the idea of *Person.*   In
our statement, it is made to apply only to *the Son,* in
whom alone " dwelleth the fullness of the Godhead
bodily," and who thus furnishes us with the only definite idea of God ; but who is no more *personal* than
the Infinite Spirit.   By union with the Finite Principle

this Spirit is made *definite* by incarnation in *Divine Substance,* who is the Father, or Creator ; but this is not definite enough even for the *apprehension* of man, much less for his comprehension. By descending through the Father to the Son, it is made still *more* definite by incarnation in a *spiritual substance,* which is still more external ; and the *possibility* arises of its communication to Human Nature. Even then, however, this communication could not have been made unless the Son had taken this nature upon, and made it *one with,* himself by his incarnation *in flesh ;* and presented us with a definite object of worship in Jesus, the Son of God, and at the same time the Son of Man, as King, Prophet, and Priest, through whom alone we can approach towards God, — and who is the witness, exponent, or representative of God to man both in a natural and in a spiritual sphere of consciousness. It is therefore written, " This is he that came by Water, and Blood, even Jesus Christ ; not by Water alone, but by Water and Blood. And it is the Spirit which beareth witness because the Spirit is Truth. For there are three that bear record in Heaven, the Father, the Word, and the Holy Ghost : and these three are one. And there are three that bear witness in Earth, the Spirit, the Water, and the Blood : and these three agree in one."

It must be at once seen that by " the Father, the Word, and the Holy Ghost," is here meant the *Divine*

Trinity or Tri-Personality in which God exists in an *Infinite sphere* of consciousness; and that by "the Spirit, the Water, and the Blood," is meant a *Spiritual* Trinity or Tri-Personality in Christ as the representative or *witness* of God, and through whom God exists in a *Finite sphere* of consciousness, constituting a *Divine-Human* or *Spiritual* sphere.   This supplies a middle ground or mediating principle in which God and Man may meet in harmonious recognition; and from which man can, by becoming receptive of the Spiritual, which is *one with* the Divine, be translated through regeneration from a Natural to a Spiritual existence; and become united to God by becoming conscious of *the same kind of life,* and so capable of conscious communion with Him, and conscious direction from Him.

With the three Personalities, or Spheres of Life, which constitute the Divine Trinity, and belong to *an Infinite sphere of consciousness,* therefore, we have nothing to do, except as we find them manifested in Christ; because, a *finite creature* cannot become conscious from *an infinite point of view.*   Our worship is not to be divided between three persons, but confined to *one person.*   This person is "*Emanuel*," who is "*God with us,*" and manifests, *through one form, Three Divine Persons,* or Personalities, which we call a Trinity of Father, Son, and Holy Ghost, — and which, by being brought down into a Spiritual or Divine-Human sphere, are

made comprehensible to us. If we had not first obtained a statement of Tri-Personality, however, there
could be no life or spiritual significance in any statement we should make of the Trinity as existing in
Christ, the Emanuel, or God with us ; or any comprehension of that Divine-Human sphere, to the contemplation of which we are now led. As to the word
person, we are not acquainted with any term that could
well be substituted for this to express those Individual-
izations into which the Godhead is evidently separable ;
nor do we see any necessity for such substitution.

TRINITY

THE LAW OF SALVATION.

HAVING shown the necessity that God should exist as a Three-fold Personality *as the condition of creation,* I will now proceed to show the necessity that God should assume Human Nature, or become incarnated in Flesh, *as the consequence* of creation, and *as the condition of Salvation* to mankind.

All things in Heaven having been reconciled to the Father by the sacrifice of the Son, so that the external was made one with the internal, a Divine Trinity realized, and a heavenly sphere established, — *creation became possible ;* and if God had determined that this creation should be simply *natural,* and so in every sense *necessitated,* — supposing such a creation possible, — this incarnation would not have been necessary, and indeed could not have taken place. It would not have been *necessary,* because the salvation of man by being made at-one with God, — which was the object to be accomplished by it, — would of course have been out of the question from the impossibility of his ever becoming conscious of or receptive from the Spiritual. It could not have *taken place*, because no union between Spiritual and Natural principles, and so no incarnation, could possibly have been effected, for the want of some connecting link by which they could be united.

For the same reasons, however, we may see that a merely natural creation would have been impossible; and thus we learn, both from the Scriptures and from the known structure and functions of the human soul, — which as the *head* of creation must determine the condition of all that is relatively *body*, — that the creation, — which constitutes the "*things in earth*" alluded to in the Trinitarian formula just quoted, — was designed by God to be a *spiritual* creation; and thus to become *reconciled* to or made *at-one* with him, instead of existing separated from and unconsciously *opposed* to him. It is therefore that he said "Let us make man in our image, after our likeness."

In consequence of this determination, and as the only means of accomplishing this design, man was created *both Natural and Spiritual*. Besides his earthy natural existence, subject to the laws of growth, decay, and decomposition, which was necessary *as a basis* for his individuality; man was endowed with *the capacity* for realizing a *spiritual* nature, of which this earthy nature was representative or symbolic. There was implanted in him, *as seed*, a spiritual principle which, after the lapse of time necessary for the growth of all his natural powers, should spring up within him, and bear to him the fruit of eternal life or of eternal death, as he should use or abuse the liberty that must then be entrusted to him as a spiritual being. In this way it was provided that a spiritual nature should become developed in man which should serve as a medium for the realization of an order of experiences *identical in character with the experiences of God,* although infinitely removed in capacity, so that when this medium of communication with him should be opened in man, God could say, as we read in the Scriptures, *" Behold, the man is become as one of us,* to know Good and Evil." This spiritual experience must from its nature include a distinct and perfect recognition, or consciousness, of those Infinite and Finite forces which constitute the substance of Good and of Evil, — of Life and of Death, — an experience that is accompanied both by the capacity and the necessity of choosing between these opposite principles, so that a state of freedom may be realized, and a sacrifice of self-ism consummated in man that shall make him at-one with the Infinite Principle of Life, precisely as the Father and the Son were made one with it as the condition of Tri-Personality and of Creation ; for this we have seen, in our statement of the Law of Trinity, to be the universal Law of

14

Spiritual Life. By this sacrifice man would be redeemed, not only from the *unconscious* opposition to
God which inheres in him as a natural production, —
or as a creature produced by infinite force from a finite
substance, possessing a finite character, and animated
by a finite self-ism, or self-love ; — but also from a
conscious opposition, resulting in condemnation or
damnation, which would take place upon *the rejection*
of Good and the acceptance of Evil as the future law
of his being. I say, man by this sacrifice of the cross
would be redeemed from death both in a natural and in
a spiritual sense, and become at-one with or reconciled
to God, — a partaker of his nature, — and a sharer in
his glory and blessedness. *The head* of creation having
become reconciled to God, all lower phenomena which
constitute *the body* of creation would become reconciled
with him, because the condition of the body is entirely
dependent upon that of the head, and takes from
this its form and character, as we have already seen
in illustrating the formation of a Tri-Personality in
God.

The *possibility* of such a capacity in man, and such a
redemption for him, as we have now described, is a
great mystery that can never be perfectly comprehended.
The *facts*, however, we can never be allowed to doubt,
because, rationally considered, creation would otherwise
have been impossible ; and because, if we deny this, we
pronounce Christianity to be a delusion, or an imposture,

and virtually acknowledge that like brutes we live, and like brutes, also, we are to perish.

Now the fact that man was created with this capacity, and for this end, *necessitated the Incarnation.* It became necessary, in order that man should realize the design of his creation, that *the Son,* as the most external sphere of existence, or form of personality in God, should, " *in the fullness of time,"* — that is, after a human sphere had been completed, and human nature as a natural production had, in the progress of the ages, attained to its full and perfect development, — descend into this atmosphere in the form of a man.

He must have been born into *this atmosphere,* because, as the experience of man must have *a body,* as well as *a soul* and *a spirit,* as the condition of a perfect or spiritual realization, — and as this, being the lowest atmosphere, *corresponds* with body, — here must be laid the foundation of all of which he can ever become conscious.

He must have been born in *the fullness of time,* because a *Divine-Human* sphere could not have been formed until a *Human* sphere, the development of which must occupy this full period of time, had been completed and become fit for union with a *Divine* sphere. Human nature could not before this have attained to a complete development, and so could not have been prepared for regeneration into a form of Divine Humanity, which was the end of its creation, because *generation must precede regeneration,* and that this is not instantaneous, but is the work of many ages, we shall prove both from the Scriptures, and from known phenomena in the history of human nature.

St. Paul has therefore taught, "That was not first which is spiritual, but that which is natural; and afterwards that which is spiritual. The first man is of the earth, earthy. The second man is the Lord from Heaven." If born *previous* to this, the human race, — not being prepared for his reception, and being constituted as antagonistic, — could not have been affected by him except in being excited to *oppose* and *destroy* him; so that his rejection, and the consequent destruction of the soul, must inevitably have resulted; a fact that was *represented* in the rejection of Christ by the Jews and the destruction of their temple and their nationality. If born *after* this, it would have been too late; because the soul would already have been destroyed by the finite force of which it must at this period become conscious.

He must have been born *in the form of a man,* not only because this is the highest form of natural existence, but because *the object* of the incarnation was to make Human Nature *as body* one with the Divine Nature *as soul* by its regeneration and glorification as Divine-Human; so that a sphere of Absolute Existence might be realized from which man could be sustained in a spiritual consciousness intellectually, affectionally, and actively. This could of course be accomplished only by the union of these two natures in one individual who would thus be both Divine and Human, — both God and Man, — constituting him a mediator or medium of communication between them.

Three principal causes, then, seem to present themselves to our consideration as necessitating the Incarnation; first, the formation of a Divine-Human sphere of life ; — second, the provision of experiences for man that should be suggestive of the Spiritual ; — and third, the provision of experiences in God of the imperfections and evils incident to Human Nature.

In the first place, the Incarnation was necessary as the means of providing for the formation of a Divine-Human sphere of life. It is to be premised that man is not an absolute principle of Life, or portion of Divine Substance, — as the Pagan philosophers taught, and as their Unitarian followers now believe, — but is only *a creature,* or material creation. That is, that he is simply an organ, receptacle, or medium, suited to the production of certain *phenomena ;* — first, of those which are natural, relative, and apparent, and afterwards, of those which are spiritual, absolute, and real. Consequently, that he is dependent for the sustenance and support of his being upon *influx* from spheres of *absolute existence.* Now so long as man remained natural, — which was until he had completed the development of all his natural powers, — the incarnation was not necessary ;

because, like all other natural things, he could then be
sustained by an infinite, and supported by a finite
force, and this would make the continuation of his life
possible.   The reason is this.   Although the soul could
not become *conscious* of infinite and finite force without
demanding the sacrifice of one or of the other, which
in either case would be fatal to it because *both* are
necessary to its life ; — as the natural cannot become
conscious of anything that is real or absolute, but only
of what is apparent or phenomenal, it must remain
perfectly *unconscious* of the operation of these absolute
spiritual causes, both of which could, therefore, continue
to act upon it in producing effects or appearances harmonious with and representative of themselves.   It is
this that constitutes the natural principle what it is
represented in the Scriptures to be, — "the tree of the
knowledge of good and evil in the midst of the garden."
But when, instead of being a natural appearance, man
should have become a spiritual reality by the unfolding,
in the fullness of time, of a spiritual nature in him
capable of absolute cognition, — when he should have
become conscious as a personal experience of the nature
of those absolute opposites from which he had been
receptive, and have surrendered himself, as he must, to
one or to the other, absolutely and eternally, — the
destruction of the soul would have been the consequence : for, whether it should choose an infinite or a
finite law as the force under the operation of which it

should come, the dissipation of its existence would become inevitable for reasons already considered in describing the effects of spiritual and material Pantheism. Hence the necessity arises that a sphere of absolute existence should be formed in which the Human principle, — designated in the Scriptures as *flesh*, as *earth*, and as *land*, — should be made one with an opposite Divine principle, so that the soul could be both sustained and supported by the operation of infinite and finite force *coming to it through a medium in which these had not only been reconciled and united, but also in which they had been made one with the Natural principle.* This union of spiritual and natural principles in a Divine-Human sphere, — as well as the justification and regeneration of the human soul, which was thereby rendered possible, — is, therefore, *prophesied* in the following passage from Isaiah : —

" The spirit of the Lord God is upon me ; because the Lord hath anointed me to preach good tidings unto the meek ; he hath sent me to bind up the broken hearted, to proclaim liberty to the captives, and the opening of the prison to them that are bound.

" To proclaim the acceptable year of the Lord, and the day of vengeance of our God ; to comfort all that mourn ; to give unto them beauty for ashes, the oil of joy for mourning, the garment of praise for the spirit of heaviness ; that they might be called trees of righteousness, the planting of the Lord, that might be glorified.

"I will rejoice greatly in the Lord, my soul shall be joyful in my God; for he hath clothed me with the garments of salvation, he hath covered me with the robe of righteousness, as a bridegroom decketh himself with ornaments, and as a bride adorneth herself with her jewels. For as the earth bringeth forth her bud, and as the garden causeth the things that are sown in it to spring forth; so the Lord God will cause righteousness and praise to spring forth before all the nations.

"For Zion's sake will I not hold my peace, and for Jerusalem's sake will I not rest, until the righteousness thereof go forth as brightness, and the salvation thereof as a lamp that burneth.

"And the Gentiles shall see thy righteousness, and all kings thy glory: and thou shalt be called by *a new name*, which the mouth of the Lord shall name. Thou shalt also be a crown of glory in the hand of the Lord, and a royal diadem in the hand of thy God. Thou shalt no more be termed *Forsaken*; neither shall *thy land* any more be termed *Desolate*: but thou shalt be called, The object of my delight; and thy land the wedded matron: for the Lord delighteth in thee and thy land shall be married. For as a young man weddeth a virgin, so shall thy restorer wed thee: and as the bridegroom rejoiceth in his bride, so shall thy God rejoice in thee."

In the second place, the Incarnation was necessary as the means of providing experiences for man that should be suggestive of the spiritual. According to a universal law of Being already recognized in our statement of the Law of Duality, production is not possible without the union of an external with an internal, as well as an affectional with an intellectual principle. A double necessity, therefore, existed *in the condition of the soul* for the Incarnation. While it was necessary, in the first place, that a Divine-Human sphere might be originated, from which the soul could be sustained and supported as a spiritual existence by an influx of spiritual life ; it was equally necessary, in the second place, that a ground of *sensible experiences* might be originated that should be *suggestive* of this spiritual life, and furnish an external principle, as *body*, in which this internal principle, as *soul*, could become incarnated as a living, active, and productive power, by which its salvation and regeneration could be effected. It is therefore written, — "How shall they believe in him of whom they have not heard ? and how shall they hear without a preacher ? and how shall they preach except they be sent ? as it is written, How beautiful are the feet of them that preach the gospel of peace, and bring glad tidings of good things ! So then, Faith cometh by hearing, and hearing by the Word of God."

This sensible experience, as *the letter* of spirituality, could be provided for man only by "*the Word of God*," incarnated in Flesh ; — by the life and teaching of Jesus upon earth, who, as both God and Man, united in him-

15

self all spiritual and all natural things as internal and external, made one as soul and body by the regeneration of the external principle. This experience has been transmitted to us through the Scriptures of the New Dispensation, and through the Churches which he established upon the earth ; containing traditions, rites, observances, doctrines, and sacraments, which he will preserve as the ground out of which the Divine Seed will spring for all time, — furnishing a suggestive principle through the means of which *spiritual ideas* derived by intuition, or inspiration, can be realized to the soul in forms of *spiritual thought.*

It is true that this external experience is not *immediately* productive of spiritual fruit, as the grossly natural condition of the *Christian world,* as we in popular language term it, would seem abundantly to indicate. The reason for this is, that a *spiritual natural* principle must first be provided in the individual soul as *a ground* out of which the *spiritual itself* may be born to it ; it being necessary, under the Law of Individuality, that everything should be provided not only with a physical basis as Body, but also with a natural basis as Soul, before a spiritual birth can be realized to it, or its regeneration effected. And by spiritual natural we mean a principle, that, while being natural, and thus discordantly diversified, is, at the same time, *representative of the spiritual ;* as if a *spiritual soul* were united to, without being made one with, a *natural body ;* between which, therefore, although spiritually or absolutely antagonistic, there is still a natural apprehensive attraction through feeling.

By *the first coming* of the Lord, an external natural experience *representative* of the Spiritual is furnished, which, by uniting with an internal natural or sentimental experience harmonious with it, produces a ground of thought, affection, and activity also *representative* of the Spiritual, and which the Soul *supposes to be* spiritual. This becomes part and parcel of the individual character, and is made one with the individual in the several spheres of his natural consciousness, and with all the various principles of his nature. Hence the great diversity in religious belief, resulting from the different positions of individuals ; and the multitude of different and differing denominations into which the Church has always been divided. This diversity would not of course be if the Church were really spiritual ; for, although the Catholic Church, as the most perfect *external representative* of Christianity, must represent the unity or universality which is inseparable from the spiritual, — and is enabled to do this by enforcing its claim to infallibility, and excluding the operation of individual thought, — this Church is, as we shall show, not *less* natural for this, but *more* so, as what it gains in *the form* of spirituality it loses in nearness to *the substance.* This fact is exemplified in the whole progress of the Church, as it passes from Catholic to Protestant, — from Trinitarian to Unitarian, — and from Unitarian to Tran-

scendental ; — from which, as the extreme bound of the
Natural, it must either return to Catholicism, or ascend
into Spiritualism.　Although there is here a continually
accelerated vastation or dissipation of that which *repre-
sents* the spiritual, there is a corresponding approach
towards the *spiritual itself*, and preparation for its reception.　It is only after all these have been passed through
that the Spiritual itself can be realized ; for that " the
first shall be last, and the last shall be first," is a law of
spiritual life, of which the rejection of the Jews and the
bringing in of the Gentiles was illustrative, and the following language of Isaiah prophetic : —

" Lebanon shall be turned into a fruitful field, and the
fruitful field shall be esteemed as a forest.　And in that
day shall the deaf hear the words of the. Book, and the
eyes of the blind shall see out of obscurity and out of
darkness.　They also that erred in spirit shall come to
understanding, and they that murmured shall learn
doctrine.　They that destroyed thee shall become thy
builders ; and they that laid thee waste shall become
thine offspring.　And they shall build up the old
wastes, they shall raise up the former desolations, and
they shall repair the waste cities, the desolations of
many generations.　And strangers shall stand and feed
your flocks, and the sons of the alien shall be your
ploughmen and vine-dressers.　I am sought of them
that asked not for me ; I am found of them that sought
me not : I said behold me ! behold me ! unto a nation

that was not called by my name. I will therefore call them my people which were not my people, and her beloved which was not beloved. And it shall come to pass, that in the place where it was said unto them, Ye are not my people, there shall they be called the children of the Living God."

It is only, then, at the *second coming* of the Lord, that the external teaching of Christ and his Apostles, as perpetuated in the Scriptures and in the Churches which he established, becomes productive of genuine spiritual results ; — it is only when the representative truths which have been realized to the soul through the means of a union between its sentimental experiences and its external teaching become suggestive of and are united to an *Absolute Divine Intelligence,* communicated to the soul through the spiritual understanding in laws of spiritual life, — that those absolute spiritual experiences can be realized by which Salvation and Regeneration are effected. Then, " with open face beholding as in a glass the Glory of the Lord, we are changed into the same image from glory to glory even as by the Spirit of the Lord."

In the third place, the Incarnation was necessary as the means of providing experiences for God. Be not offended, reader, at so hard a saying. God being himself Absolute Law, cannot be exempt from the operation of laws which constitute his own Being. That consciousness and identity are inseparable we have seen to be an established law of existence; and this being so, it is clearly evident that an experience by God of all the evils and infirmities of human nature, and their removal *in Himself*, by which the Human should become Divine, was absolutely necessary before he could *be prepared* to remove them from the *human soul* by regenerating it into an image of the Divine Humanity which he had thus established; so that as we had borne the image of the earthy, we might now bear the image of the heavenly. All this was accomplished by the Incarnation. Being an *Infinite Person*, the Son by this incarnation *necessarily* became conscious of every degree of imperfection or evil that could possibly be experienced by any individual for all eternity; and it is therefore said in the Scriptures that " *he took upon himself the sins of the whole world.*" By removing these natural imperfections or evils in himself by a regeneration of his own Human Principle, he was prepared to remove them from all those who should, through Faith, receive him, by which they should be made through him at-one with God. It is evident that these evils could not otherwise have been known to God, and so could never have been removed by him. It is therefore that Jesus said, — " For the Father judgeth no man, but has committed all judgment to the Son, *because he is the Son of Man.*" The fact of Incarnation as furnishing this necessary experience to the Son as the Saviour of mankind, as it has here been stated, is also distinctly recognized by the greatest of all the Apostles. He says, —

"Forasmuch then as the children are partakers of Flesh and Blood, he also himself likewise took part of the same ; for verily he took not upon him the nature of Angels, but he took on him the seed of Abraham. Wherefore it behooved him in all things to be made like unto his brethren, that he might be a merciful High Priest in things pertaining to God, to make reconciliation for the sins of the people."

"For we have not a High Priest who cannot be touched with a feeling of our infirmities, but was in all points tempted as we are, yet without sin."

By the statement and application of what are assumed to be the three primary laws of existence, constituting the Trinitarian Principle or Law of Tri-Personality, we have demonstrated the necessity that, as the condition of creation, God should exist as a Tri-Personality constituting three several spheres of Absolute Being, as Body, Soul, and Spirit ; and have obtained a definite statement of this Tri-Personality which *corresponds* with the teaching of the Scriptures, and *harmonizes* with that of the Church. We have also demonstrated the necessity that, as the condition of salvation to mankind, God should become incarnated in Flesh, or appear in the atmosphere of earth in the form of a man. In doing this, we have not merely demonstrated *the Divinity of Christ*, or the position of the Son as a mode of existence in God, or as a part of the personality of God; but we have demonstrated the existence of Christ as " *the Saviour*," or as " *the Emanuel* ; " who is " *God with us*," because he manifests *in his own person* a Trinity of Father, Son, and Holy Ghost. We have thus demonstrated and explained the sense of the Trinitarian formula given to us in the Scriptures by John; because we have, by the statement and application of the Law of Tri-Personality, succeeded in realizing or producing a distinct conception of the " *three that bear record in Heaven*," who constitute " *the fullness of God*," and also the " *three that bear witness in earth*," who constitute " *the fullness of the Godhead bodily*."

We are aware that many have presumed to deny the genuineness of the Trinitarian formula here alluded to. No external authority, however, can be sufficient to overthrow or to set aside the internal evidence of its truth that has here been presented. *We know* that it is genuine because it has here been *reproduced* by the application of Universal Laws of Being which are more clearly demonstrable than the simplest fact, because all created things, without a single exception, can be produced as proof. We are not now dependent upon external authority even for the support of the spiritual truths of Revelation; but are able to explain, to verify, and even to reproduce them. This conception of the modes of existence and manifestation in God will enable us to arrive at others equally clear, comprehensive, and harmonious, of all the Ideas included in Christianity, of which the doctrines or dogmas of the Church are only imperfect and discordant natural substitutes ; and, being founded in Absolute Law, which is the essence of Rationality, must remain as definite and unchangeable as those of the Church are uncertain and fluctuating. These, with the laws in which they are founded, and the conclusions to which they lead, will furnish principles of interpretation by which the internal spiritual sense of the Scriptures may be unfolded, and its Letter, — now discordant and obscure, and susceptible of all kinds of interpretation, — be made perfectly harmonious, intelligible, and determinate.

The writer deeply feels the responsibility which he assumes in thus claiming to have stated *for the first time* the only absolute and permanent, and thus the only true foundation that can possibly be laid for Ontological, Theological, and Psychological Truth, which must include the sum of all our knowledge. It is a position that nothing but the most entire and unqualified assurance of the truth and the importance of this foundation, continued and continually increasing for a series of years, because confirmed by long reflection, conscious experience, and extensive application, could induce him to take. This statement is presented by him confidently as being the only rational foundation upon which the existence of God and his peculiar attributes and relations to the human race, as these

16

have been taught in the Scriptures and recognized
by the Church, can be sustained. It is true that the
existence and attributes of God may be in some sort
proved upon Scriptural grounds, or by logical argu-
ments based upon language of the Scriptures. But
there are two very serious objections to any exclusive
reliance upon such grounds and such reasoning. In
the first place, this language is susceptible of a great
variety of interpretations, and the genuineness of pas-
sages important to the argument is very extensively
questioned. In the second place, this language can,
at the best, furnish nothing but an external dogmatic
ground of reasoning which must to *all* minds be less
satisfactory than that which is internal and self-evident,
while to *many* minds it would, unless confirmed by
other evidence, be entirely worthless. In view of these
considerations it must. be evident that a demonstration
of these great facts that shall be complete and final,
because founded in laws which, while they are self-
evident, may be illustrated, and thus demonstrated, by
reference both to the Scriptures and to all the phenomena of natural existence, must be the greatest
possible desideratum, and must lead, in truth, to " *the
end of controversy* " upon the subject of Theology.

Now although the external evidence furnished by
the phenomena of Nature, illustrating and demonstrating these laws, has not here been presented, the *internal*
evidence of their truth has been given in showing that

the cause of existence must necessarily be in exact correspondence with them. Besides this, we have shown that these identical laws have been proclaimed in the Scriptures in the most decided and unmistakable manner. We have shown that they are there established as Universal Laws according to which everything must exist ; so that the question now to be settled is not, What are the Universal Laws of Existence ? but, *How has Nature been constituted, and how is it governed in correspondence with these laws ?* Our system is to be the answer to this question. We shall there make an application of these laws, and show that their promulgation in the Scriptures is neither poetical, vague, or merely abstract, but is capable of the most extensive practical application. By this means Ontology, Theology, and Psychology, which have heretofore been so decidedly hostile to each other and so discordant in themselves, will be harmoniously united in *one system*, and their reality as *absolute science* demonstrated. In doing this we shall, as I have before said, realize PHILOSOPHY in its legitimate or absolute character as THE SCIENCE OF THINGS DIVINE AND OF THINGS HUMAN.

OCKER
MAR 2 6 1981

Lightning Source UK Ltd.
Milton Keynes UK
UKHW020634110520
363086UK00012B/903